Independent London
store guide

Effie Fotaki and Moritz Steiger

MONSTERMEDIA PUBLISHING

Independent Shoppers, We salute you!

We are proud to present the entirely new second edition of our book, Independent London store guide.

It has been interesting to see what has happened to London's high streets – especially since we all got mugged by the banks – there has been a great rise in service based shops, from wine tastings to knitting clubs or learning to recover furniture. Although the internet has had an undoubted affect, shops are offering services that cannot be achieved online. The credit crunch has also encouraged a make-do and mend approach rather than a buy it cheap, throw-away attitude. It could be seen as a positive social development.

What is also clear, is that where there is a good number of quality independent shops, the area and community tends to be a lot healthier. The streets are more vibrant with people, hanging and socialising, money going into the shops tends to stay more local. That's why we suggest you go to these areas, even if you don't find want you want, there are some interesting places to just 'hangout'.

We hope you enjoy our best book so far of the best Independent shops we could find for you, around London.

Demonstrate our usefulness and be sure to show our guide to shop owners! Don't leave home with out it.

****Look out for the in-shop offers with this book***
Be aware that some of these offers may only be on selected items and available for a limited period only.

GRIMETAPE
ASVP
Humps for
300 yards

Contents

Look mum no hands! 49 Old Street EC1 / www.lookmumnohands.com

N1 **Hoxton**

E2/EC2 **Shoreditch**

E1 **Spitalfields**

E1 **Brick Lane**

E2 **Columbia Road**

E8 **Broadway Market**

E9 **Victoria Village**

'Look mum no hands' embodies a positive trend for bringing like minded people together for things other than just drink or sports tv. In their case its headsets and gear sprockets. Great place.

BookArtBookShop

Bookartbookshop is a place for those with an obsessive love of words and paper. A unique shop that sells handmade, limited edition books made by artists and small press publishers such as Red Fox and Concrete Hermit, its range includes obscure publications on arcane subjects ranging from pataphysics to surrealism. Here you will find books of all shapes and sizes, some screen-printed, some hand-typed, some with covers made of perspex or bubble wrap and some where you won't know if it's a book or a sculpture. It's a perfect starting point for any budding illustrator to find inspiration. In addition to hosting lectures, discussions and book launches, owner Tanya wanted to devise a space to support others using the window display as an opportunity for local artists and students to show their works as well as lovingly displaying a wide range of their books and hand-printed cards and postcards. *PB*

MAP 3 Ref. 30

BookArtBookshop
17 Pitfield Street
Hoxton N1 6HB
+44 (0)20 7375 3168
www.bookartbookshop.com
Wed–Fri 11–7pm
Sat 12–6pm

Goodhood

This menswear store located on a cobbled street off Hoxton Square is where you would come to find high end Japanese streetwear brands. Here they can tell you why only the Japanese can make jeans the way they should be made and why you should settle for nothing less than a 'salvaged edge' made on an old fashioned loom (much harder wearing apparently). Goodhood stocks a range of independent streetwear designers from all over the world who only do limited runs so you are unlikely to ever find someone wearing the same piece. Matt black walls, t-shirts hung with equal spacing and a glass floor where you can spy on their design studio downstairs make **Goodhood** feel a bit like an art gallery. Their range of trendy magazines, solid silver jewellery with swan heads and skulls with Minnie Mouse ears make this store the epitome of Hoxton-cool. *PB*

MAP 3 Ref. 29
Goodhood
41 Coronet Street
Hoxton N1 6HD
+44 (0)20 7729 3600
www.goodhoodstore.co.uk
Mon–Fri 11–7pm
Sat 11–6.30pm

Sh!

What can we say! Sex shops just don't come much classier (or more kitsch) than this. Yes **Sh!** has shelves packed full with lubricants, dildos, vibrators, flavoured condoms, DVDs, books, and all manner of kinky costumes and sex aids. But with names like 'G-swirl booster', "Thrill Dill Countess" and 'Mystic Wand', it's easy to pick up a double ended dildo and forget what you're looking at. With dusty pink walls, paintings of angels, heart shaped chairs and love hearts frosted on the windows this sex shop is all about girls (on girls) and would send most men running for the nearest pint. You will find every kind of stimulant and silicon device along with feather plumes, French knickers, leather cuffs, rude candy, books of Japanese bondage and greetings cards not forgetting a sweet choice of cat-o-nine-tails for the more exotically inclined. *PB*

MAP 3 Ref. 30

Sh!
57 Hoxton Square
Hoxton N1 6PB
0845 868 9599
www. sh-womenstore.com
Mon–Sun 12–8pm

The Willow Shoreditch

On one of London's more authentic East End streets, a stone's throw from Shoreditch and nestled between a chicken shop and a newsagents, is the most stylish florist cum café you will ever hope to find. With a background of 10 years working with the likes of Alexander McQueen and Christian Louboutin, the **Willow**'s owner, Ying, knows what 'chic' should look like. The shop is divided into two halves, "flowers at the front, food at the back and things in between". All the food, the delicious salads and cakes are made fresh that morning by Ying himself. It may have been done on a shoe string, but the elegant interior, comprised of reclaimed wood and quirky furniture, with a constantly changing theme to co-ordinate with the flowers is evidence that some people just have a true knack of making something out of nothing. *PB*

MAP 3 Ref. 34
The Willow Shoreditch
92 Hoxton Street
Hoxton N1 6LP
+44 (0)20 7739 3009
www.thewillowshoreditch.com
Mon–Sun 10.30–5.30pm

7 Upholstery

So you're on your way home and you come across a well worn armchair tossed on the street, another victim of another swanky pub conversion and it occurs to you that this chair is too good to end up in the skip. Well here's a tip, take it to **7 Upholstery**, they take bespoke very seriously. Whatever you want, they will do. Although not conventional upholsterers, I mean how many of them have pale pink hair, tattoos and compare upholstery to taxidermy? Booked up 3 to 4 months in advance, their range of the best fabrics from family-run suppliers of the finest tweed, wool, quilted or patterned fabric, all to your own specification, make it well worth the wait. They specialise in refurbishing classic mid-twentieth century furniture, which can be done using original 1960's and 1970's fabric, it may be cost a premium but the results are worth it. PB

MAP 2 Ref. 18
7 Upholstery
1a Boundary Street
Shoreditch E2 7JE
+44 (0)20 7613 4925
www.7upholstery.co.uk
Tue–Fri 9–5.30pm
Sat 9.30–5pm
Sun 10.30–4.30pm

11 Boundary

A clothes boutique for the super-chic who chant the mantra "black never goes out of style". Here they have a neatly edited selection of pieces with emphasis on black, studs, leather, sequins and glass beads. **11 Boundary** is a nod to those that know their look and like to add to their ever expanding wardrobe of black and studs. You will find sleek garments in muted tones and soft fabrics by the likes of Twenty8Twelve, L.A.M.B and C'N'C Costume National. There is a good selection of shoes from Vivienne Westwood + Melissa and Sam Edelman and delicate jewellery by the likes of House of Harlow. The look of the steely fashion editor wouldn't be complete however without a pair of sunglasses by Tom Ford. *PB*

MAP 2 Ref. 17

11 Boundary
11 Boundary Street
Shoreditch E2 7JE
+44 (0)20 7033 0310
www.11boundary.com
Tue–Sat 10–7pm
except Thu 10–8pm
Sun 11–5pm

A Child of The Jago

It all started 30 years ago when a young punk from Yorkshire went to London in search of kindred spirits, only to find what he was looking for at World's End, the renowned shop owned by Malcolm McLaren and Vivienne Westwood. It was here he met their son Joe and a long lasting friendship was born. **A Child of the Jago**, aptly named after the 1896 novel depicting the violence and crime the area was prone to, came about, well, out of thin air really. With an interior like the inside of a pirate's ship or a circus tent, it doesn't have the feel of a standard shop, more of a museum where everything is for sale. Upstairs you will find hand tailored pieces made within walking distance of the shop and downstairs a collection of beautiful antique clothing, from late 1800's French cavalry jackets to Chinese circus outfits and 1940's hunting breeches. *PB*

MAP 2 Ref. 22
A Child of the Jago
10 Great Eastern Street
Shoreditch EC2A 3NT
+44 (0)20 7377 8694
www.achildofthejago.com
Mon–Sat 11–7pm
Sun 12–5pm

Bordello

One minute you're on Great Eastern Street, the next you're in a brothel on the set of an old Western film. It's as if Mae West or Bettie Page just left the room. Whether it means to or not **Bordello** reeks of nostalgia and the old movie stars. An antique bed and dressing table, dark red walls, black floor boards and draped silk curtains provoke an atmosphere of Victorian eroticism, or Dita Von Teese's dressing room. Bordello is all about getting ready for sex, it's about women dressing up for men, a sexy boudoir for girls. Owner Michelle, an ex-city banker opened Bordello as she wanted to create the fantasy shop she had in her head. The exquisite, delicate lingerie, vintage feather fans, diamante suspenders and sequinned nipple tassels don't just need to be the props of the burlesque pros! *PB*

MAP 2 Ref. 23
Bordello
55 Great Eastern Street
Shoredicth EC2A 3HP
+44 (0)20 7503 3334
www.bordello-london.com
Mon–Sat 11–7pm

The Bridge Coffee House

Now if we're talking interiors then **The Bridge** is totally unparalleled. This is one hell of a collection of stuff, seamlessly traversing across many time periods and continents. Fuchsia pink upholstered chairs mixed with framed photographs of Robert de Niro and Wild West heroes, vintage fluorescent signs, chandeliers, Tiffany lamps and exotic furniture make this the most visually exciting café I have ever seen. The owner Ricco has designed every inch himself from the door handles to the priceless collection itself, "If I see something I like and I can afford it, I buy it, I don't wait for tomorrow, you have to have a passion". Well The Bridge certainly has passion. The delicious coffee and selection of over-the-top creamy cakes make this the perfect spot to while away the time, although don't go if keeping eye contact is required, it's all just too distracting. *PB*

MAP 2 Ref. 32

The Bridge Coffee House
15 Kingsland Road
Shoreditch E2 8AA
+44 (0)20 3489 2216
Mon–Wed 8–1am
Thu–Sat 8–2am
Sun 10–12am

An interior stylist by trade, **Caravan**'s owner Emily loves collecting and arranging things, "opening a shop seemed like the natural thing to do, a girl having a shop is like a boy having a shed!". Here you will find something in every price bracket to embellish your home, from shabby chic glass candle-holders to pretty jewellery boxes and vintage teapots. Emily sells things, which give personality to an environment - you can tell she is extremely house-proud. Whether it's a wooden coat hook in the shape of a deer head or hand-printed trompe l'oeil wallpaper creating the illusion of floor to ceiling bookshelves, 'it's all about decorating a dwelling' she says. There are all kinds of quirky things: plastic ravens, rabbit shaped lamps not forgetting the concrete sheep, and lots of glass domes in different sizes. For me Caravan is the perfect gift shop. *PB*

MAP 2 Ref. 20
Caravan
3 Redchurch Street
Shoreditch E2 7DJ
+44 (0)20 7033 3532
www.caravanstyle.com
Tue–Fri 11–6.30pm
Sat–Sun 12–6pm

The Grocery

On a stretch of land, pretty much solely inhabited by Vietnamese restaurants, was launched the **Grocery** because as the owner puts it, 'there was nowhere to buy food round here'. Here they make doing your weekly food shop fun. You feel healthy just setting foot in the place. The exposed brick walls and shelves stacked with 12 different types of organic sugar, remind you how much fun cooking can be. Although it may be mis-construed as somewhat pretentious, they don't care. For healthy types there is nothing you won't find here, from every different kind of gluten free flour to organic vegetables. They even stock an extensive range of hair and beauty products whereby you will never go to Boots again. Now if the deli section wasn't satisfying enough there is a café tucked away at the back with big country kitchen style wooden tables and copies of The Guardian strewn about, serving the best coffee and delicious food from homemade soup to quiche and fancy scrambled eggs. *PB*

MAP 2 Ref. 33

The Grocery
54-58 Kingsland Road
ShoreditchE2 8DP
+44 (0)20 7729 6855
www.thegroceryshop.co.uk
Mon–Sun 8–10pm

Hostem

Black Hessian lines the walls of this sartorial boutique mixing eclectic and modern menswear with "Goth Drapery", avant-garde clothes with impeccable style, quality and finish in varying shades of black. The elegant, worn aesthetic of the store houses streetwear inspired brands for those that 10 years ago wore Stussy but are now more inclined to wear Adam Kimmel or Mastermind Japan. Semi-bespoke beautifully tailored pieces from the likes of Rik Owens, Damir Doma and Ann Demeulemeester and rails of black jumpers in various different cuts, shades and fabrics complete the store's 'grown-up concept'. With previous experience running the Dover Street Market, **Hostem** is run by men who know and love fashion and the pieces come at a price which reflects the product and the attention to detail. *PB*

MAP 2 Ref. 16
Hostem
41–43 Redchurch Street
Shoreditch E2 7DJ
+44 (0)20 7739 9733
www.hostem.co.uk
Tue–Sat 11–7pm
Sun 12–5pm

Labour and Wait

Buying the most boring household items has never been so fun. **Labour and Wait** specialise in timeless homewares, traditional and simple, right down to the enamel lampshades and unbleached cotton oven gloves. Purchasing a dustpan and brush has taken on a whole new slant! Tired of buying cheap disposable items destined for the garbage after only a few uses, the owners decided to compile and sell everything you need for your home – useful things that will last, probably outlasting you. With a cool calm atmosphere and shelves stacked with an art gallery aesthetic, from enamel coffee pots and bread tins to horsehair brooms, linen dishtowels and old-fashioned school notebooks you can come back time and again, safe in the knowledge that you will always find what you saw last time you were there. *PB*

MAP 2 Ref. 14
Labour and Wait
85 Redchurch Street
Shoreditch E2 7DJ
+44 (0)20 7729 6253
www.labourandwait.co.uk
Tue–Sun 11–6pm

Lifestylebazaar

So you need a few basic items, some door hooks, a clock, a few plates or a birthday present perhaps? Well **Lifestyle Bazaar** will sort you out, here you will find a product designer's playground, it's like a mini museum of ideas, how to take the utilitarian and make it an art piece. Don't be intimated by the recycled paper clocks, or the wonders that can be made out of ceramic and glass as it may look expensive but is in fact very affordable. The owners understand that interior design shops can be alienating but here they have a whole wealth of things that you never knew you couldn't live without. Like a designer homeware version of an Italian Deli piled high with exotic food but in their case glass vase fridge magnets, designer chopping boards and Japanese style lunch boxes. *PB*

MAP 2 Ref. 31
Lifestyle Bazaar
11a Kingsland Road
Shoreditch E2 8AA
+44 (0)20 7739 9427
www.lifestylebazaar.com
Tue–Sat 11–7pm
Sun 12–5pm

Maiden

With a long history in museum retail, owner Noah has created a design gift shop that doesn't take itself too seriously. Here you will find witty cards and fridge magnets stacked on top of an old 60's ironing board and pulp fiction novels piled high on an iron garden bench. There isn't a particular theme as such, just random stuff you don't need but really really want, be it a mask of Charlie Chaplin or a book on Yves Saint Laurent - he just wants you to laugh your way around the shop. Noah likes to think of it as an Aladdin's cave where he is Aladdin and does everything from choose what he sells to sweeping the floor. "I like to walk into a shop and see things that I can afford" he says, so you won't have a problem finding a gift as pricetags range from anywhere between 80p to £200. *PB*

MAP 2 Ref. 21

Maiden
188 Shoreditch High Street
Shoreditch E1 6HU
+44 (0)20 7998 0185
www.maidenshop.com
Mon–Sat 11–7pm

Milk

In a unique eighteenth century building on Shoreditch's main thoroughfare is **Milk**, a 'concept boutique' owned by a couple who love to travel, a fact reflected in their eclectic taste and choice of international designers. They call it a concept boutique because each brand has a concept behind it, whether it's perfume from Laura Tonatto, described in Italy as the most highly esteemed Italian nose having created innovative fragrances for 20 years, or shoes by Repetto one of the oldest makers of ballet shoes in the world. A brilliant collection of quirky modern designs most notably by Fornasetti the Italian sculptor whose trademark is the distinctive motif of operetta soprano Lina Cavalieri's face printed on everything from porcelain plates to cushions. They sell pieces they love, focusing on small furniture items catering for the small spaces people inhabit in London, including inspired handcrafted lighting, whimsical coffee tables and umbrella stands. *PB*

MAP 2 Ref. 27
Milk
118½ Shoreditch High Street
Shoreditch E1 6JN
+44 (0)20 7729 9880
www.milkconceptboutique.eu
Mon–Fri 11–7pm
Thu 11–8pm
Sat 11–6pm
Sun 10.30–6pm

-10%

*Discount on fashion items only**

Present

Finding the best of the best seems to be the theme here. There may be a few menswear stores in Shoreditch these days but none draws you in like **Present**. Whether it's the smell of fresh coffee from London based company, Square Mile, brewed by the 2009 world barista champion, or the scent of candles from France's oldest candle maker, Cire Trudon, for one reason or another your senses will compel you to take a look.
A cathedral-like space with tall ceilings, it has custom-made, concrete-like floors and counter tops with pristine white display cabinets and aluminium shelving, all styled to perfection.
They don't buy what they think will sell, they just buy what they think is the best, they reckon to have all bases covered. With clothes and bags from Comme Des Garcons and Heritage Research, sunglasses by Rayban, shoes by Vans and products from Aesop, they know a thing or two about quality. *PB*

MAP 2 Ref. 24
Present
140 Shoreditch High Street
Shoreditch E1 6JE
+44 (0)20 7033 0500
www.present-london.com
Mon–Fri 10.30–7pm
Sat 11–6.30pm
Sun 11–5pm

Riad Yima

With elaborate lanterns hanging from the ceiling, dynamic floor mats adorning every square inch and vivid shopping bags lining the shelves, it's only after several minutes that you begin to realise that what you're looking at is in fact recycled plastic bags, used food cans and old grain sacks. Alongside his own work including coffee tables made out of Moroccan pop art Plexiglas signs and thoughtful wall pieces combining capitalistic logos and ethnic imagery, Moroccan born owner, Hassan has shown how recycling can be turned into an art. A photographer by trade he has filled his shop with beautiful and colourful housewares all made in Morocco and all made from discarded products. Be it a lamp that used to be a coffee can or a huge cushion previously a traditional rug, everything is unique and a work of art. **Riad Yima** shows Africa's ingenuity for recycling. *PB*

MAP 2 Ref. 15
Riad Yima
30–32 Calvert Avenue
Shoreditch E2 7JP
www.hassanhajjaj.com

Start

When it comes to fashion, **Start** stocks the absolute best of everything. From the moment you walk in the door and get a whiff of Comme des Garçons perfume you are hooked. The clothes are a perfect cross of Joan Jet rock-cool from Helmut Lang and Rik Owens to classic Halston and beautiful, delicate Richard Nicoll – all examples of impeccable tailoring. The store is elegant but the emphasis is really on the stock - they have an extensive range of one off pieces including the latest Melissa shoes, Diptyque perfume and sexy mafia-bride jewellery with gold studs, heavy gold chains and huge gems. Start, consistently gets it right. With a womenswear and a menswear store opposite, they always appear to be one step ahead of the trend featuring every relevant designer of the moment with sublime window displays and flawless service from staff who know what they're talking about. *PB*

MAP 2 Ref. 25

Start
42-44 Rivington Street
Shoreditch EC2A 3QQ
+44 (0)20 7729 3344
www.start-london.com
Mon–Fri 10.30–6.30pm
Sat 11–6pm
Sun 1–5pm

Sunspel

Purveyors of some of the finest underwear and staple clothing, British company **Sunspel** have been providing the most dapper English gentleman with cotton vests and boxer shorts for 150 years. The store on fashionable Redchurch Street is the personification of understated elegance and sophistication, with solid wood floors, teal coloured walls and straw boaters hung artfully on the wall, a nod to a long established client base. Sunspel specialise in jersey and Long Staple Egyptian Cotton grown only on the banks of the Nile. The recent addition of luxurious two-fold cotton highly prized around the world cements Sunspel as suppliers of pure luxury. They collaborate with many well known designers including Paul Smith and Margaret Howell, have a cameo in the famous Levi's 'launderette' advert where the model removes his jeans to reveal Sunspel boxer shorts and have produced bespoke t-shirts for Christian Bale in 'Batman The Dark Knight'. *PB*

MAP 2 Ref. 19
Sunspel
7 Redchurch Street
Shoreditch E2 7DJ
+44 (0)20 7739 9729
www.sunspel.com
Mon–Sat 11–7pm
Sun 12–6pm

The Three Threads

Located in the heart of Shoreditch, a group of friends decided to open a store combining their passion for clothing, art and beer, henceforth **The Three Threads** was born. The name comes from a London beer first served at the Bell Brew-house on Curtain Road in the early 1700s. The theme is carried on through the sophisticated bar-style fit of the shop with low lighting and an old juke box making a nice touch. What clothing store can claim to have their own brand of beer brewed specially by a local micro brewery, free to customers? There is a strong graphic element to the shop with their sweet selection of graphic tees and ever changing T-shirt wall at the back of the store. Stocking an extensive collection of streetwear for men from Edwin to Carhartt and only the best for women including Paul and Joe Sister and Opening Ceremony – the girls will certainly be happy too. *PB*

MAP 2 Ref. 24
The Three Threads
47-49 Charlotte Road
Shoreditch EC2A 3QT
+44 (0)20 7749 0503
www.thethreethreads.com
Mon–Sat 11–7pm
Sun 12–5pm

A142

From their base in an old button factory, close to Hoxton Square, what was once a mere fashion wholesalers is now one of Shoreditch's most fashionable stores. Home to some classy brands such as Designer's Remix, Twisted Vintage and By Zoe, the owners of **A142** hand-selected the collection from designers around the world, tastefully combining a few vintage pieces along with a collection of original artwork. This bright and airy space has a gallery vibe and lends itself as a perfect space to showcase their selection. They make putting the store together on a whim sound so easy, "we were already an office and showroom so putting in a front door wasn't a big stretch". It doesn't look that simple though, with custom sprayed lime-green clothes rails, scrap metal trestles, old stainless steel school lockers and paper butterflies creatively decorating the wall, it's certainly a classy showroom. Now with further ease they have moved a step closer to the high street opening a store in Old Spitalfields Market. *PB*

MAP 1 Ref. 3
A142
17 Lamb Street
Shoreditch E1 6EA
+44 (0)20 7377 8926
www.a142store.com
Mon – Sat 11 – 7pm
Sun 11 – 6pm

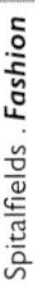

Androuet

A cheese shop just wouldn't be a cheese shop without the ripe scent of Camembert now would it? Parisian born owner, Alexandre has a long love affair with cheese. Having travelled the world exploring food, he came to London, finally opening his own shop. **Androuet** source cheese from all over the world, with 40% coming from Britain alone and all of which is bought directly from the producer. Selling only seasonal cheese they are the only shop in London who don't sell goats cheese in December or January. The restaurant, which has a selective seasonal menu featuring 'cheese of the week' dishes, features, come the winter, the traditional French favourites, Fondue and Raclette - rare to find outside of the Alps. Although mainly specialists in cheese they have enlisted the help of assistant sommelier to Gordon Ramsey to help choose the perfect selection of wines to compliment the diverse range. *PB*

MAP 1 Ref. 4
Androuet
Old Spitalfields Market
107b Commercial Street
Spitalfields E1 6BG
+44 (0)20 7375 3168
www.androuet.co.uk
Tue–Fri 11–8pm
Sat –Sun 11–7pm

Keep Zero Gravity is an independent boutique solely distributing the ethereal creations of Greek designer Ioanna Kourbella. After Ioanna's success in Greece, the owners wanted to introduce her to the British market place. Her delicate and refined garments use as few seams and stitches as possible thereby creating clothes that are designed to fit the body perfectly. Ioanna grew up in Athens observing one of a kind, hand-knitted pieces produced in her father's workshop. Her interest in tailoring developed and she went on to study fashion, costume and theatre design and was an early pioneer of using state-of-the-art textiles, made of natural fibres. The chic, simple design of the shop by a Greek theatre designer, offers a relaxing antidote to the colourful madness of Brick Lane. Additionally each month they invite a local artist to create an installation in the window as well as monthly design competitions in collaboration with Ioanna's designs. *PB*

MAP 1 Ref. 5

Keep Zero Gravity
20 Hanbury Street
Spitalfields E1 6QR
+44 (0)20 7247 5553
www.keepzerogravity.co.uk
Mon–Sun 11–7pm

The Lollipop Shoppe

The Lollipop Shoppe has a sweet eye for design! You might think you are in a kind of design sweet shop, a sweet shop selling beautifully designed products for the home, and I'm talking Verner Panton and Arne Jacobsen, not to mention Le Corbusier thrown in for good measure. Their theme is beautiful things. Classic and contemporary Scandinavian design seems to take precedence with Eames coathangers and Paul Henningsen lighting included. Concept pieces such as Piet Hein's 'super-elliptical' table where all sitters have equal importance and furniture, which experiments with bent wood and lamination are a joy for those with an interest in product design. It's not all big investment stuff though as the top floor is an eclectic selection of candles by Keith Haring, tinned sweets by Andy Warhol and multi-coloured headphones and watches interspersed with original artwork by Anthony Burrill and plastic pieces by Vasa, described as the most sensational colourist working in plastic today. *PB*

MAP 1 Ref. 2
The Lollipop Shoppe
10 Lamb Street
Spitalfields E1 6EA
+44 (0)20 7655 4540
www.thelollipopshoppe.co.uk
Mon–Sat 10–6pm
Sun 11-5pm

Precious

Opened by Kate, a former buyer for Harrods and Harvey Nichols, **Precious** is an elegant old-style boutique where the shop assistants are on a first name basis with their clientele. When you're having a crisis moment with nothing to wear, Precious will come to your rescue with their one-to-one styling service. Here you will get expert help in a peaceful, carpeted and gently lit environment from a choice of hand-selected key pieces from the current season including Diane von Furstenberg, Moschino, See by Chloe and Alexander McQueen. And it doesn't stop there. Precious offer a service for the busy city girl where they will happily bike something to you if you're suddenly stuck for a party outfit. Or need a gift perhaps? Precious stocks perfume, bath essence and candles by independent perfumer Angela Flanders who just so happens to be Kate's mother, there's nothing like keeping it in the family. *PB*

MAP 1 Ref. 1
Precious
16 Artillery Passage
Spitalfields E1 7LJ
+44 (0)20 7392 9686
www.precious-london.com
Mon–Fri 11–6.30pm
Sat 11–5pm

14 Bike Co.

There was once a time when a fixed gear bike was something exotic for only the most foolhardy cyclist. Now it's almost as easy as buying a pint of milk. **14 Bike Co.** owners John and Duncan saw a gap in the market for quality custom made fixed gear bikes. All their frames are handmade in their own workshop with parts coming from the finest suppliers. In addition, from their website you can design your own bike right down to the colour of the hubs, the store also features a 'sit and fit' service to measure your exact size requirements. They also have their own clothing label designed specifically for keen cyclists but wouldn't be out of place in a smart mens boutique and their collaboration with expert bag designers, San Francisco based Mission Workshop, make 14 Bike Co. one of the best bike shops around. *PB*

MAP 1 Ref. 6
14 Bike Co.
13 Ely's Yard
The Truman Brewery
Spitalfields E1 6QL
+44 (0)20 7377 7522
www.14bikeco.com
Mon–Fri 11–7pm
Sat –Sun 11–6pm

Dragana Perisic

Hailing from Eastern Europe, **Dragana Perisic** creates versatile and ultra-feminine, fanciful clothes from dresses to evening coats designed to be worn in different ways. With detachable sleeves that make an item wearable regardless of season, or a jacket that can be reversed making it appropriate for either day or evening wear, it is obvious she has fun inventing each piece. Her collection incorporates beautiful silk cushions and craft inspired jewellery made from handstitched fabric and silver. Using materials of the highest quality including translucent jerseys, leather, opulent brocades, floaty silks and super soft cotton in delicious and subtle colours she creates one-off timeless pieces. Her attention to detail is reflected in the dark wood floors, vintage velveteen cinema chairs and 70's furniture with Suffolk puffs, little scraps of silk gathered into flower like pieces which adorn her clothes and jewellery artfully placed in jars on the floor. *PB*

MAP 1 Ref. 12

Dragana Perisic
30 Cheshire Street
Brick Lane E2 6EH
+44 (0)20 7739 4484
www.draganaperisic.com
Tue–Fri 11–6pm
Sat–Sun 11–5pm

-10%

*Discount on innovative handbags only**

Handmade Interiors

It has to be said that one of the main attractions to a sprawling cosmopolitan city is that the best of the best is brought to your doorstep. With **Handmade Interiors** you needn't go much further than Brick Lane to find some of the loveliest hand-block and screen-printed textiles from cushion covers to cooking aprons and silk Turkish Hamam towels all the way from Turkey. Their main focus is on ethnic hand-printed products, all of which are printed in owner, Piyush's, mother's workshop back in Delhi and designed by Piyush himself. Limited edition ceramic pieces are interspersed with fragrant organic olive oil soaps and hand embroidered antique Hamam textiles from the Ottoman Empire. The simple interior of the shop shows off the delicate and beautiful designs with unique ceramics from British designers and a handwoven Turkish kaftan adorning the walls. *PB*

MAP 1 Ref. 10
Handmade Interiors
10 Cheshire Street
Brick Lane E2 6EH
+44 (0)20 7729 5704
www.handmade-interiors.co.uk
Tue–Sun 11–6pm

Le Grenier

It started out as a hobby, a mere passion for all things old - but vintage clutter turned out to have quite a market for Jean-Luis, owner of chic and shambolic vintage shop **Le Grenier**. At first glance it may look like everything here is picked at random but many of the products here are collectibles and it is evident that he really knows his subject. He makes an effort to fill his shop with a mixture of what he likes but also what he knows people want. The collection is carefully sourced from flea markets all over England. Here you will find eclectic jewellery, exciting knick knacks and old record players interspersed with sixties ceramic sugar jars, full sets of tea cups piled onto classic English pieces, a Formica table or a G-plan dresser. Seventies lampshades mixed in with an old-fashioned type writer and an enamel bread bin complete the look. *PB*

MAP 2 Ref. 13
Le Grenier
146 Bethnal Green Road
Brick Lane E2 6DG
+44 (0)20 7790 7379
www.le-grenier.com
Mon–Fri 11–6pm
Wed Closed
Sat–Sun 10–6pm

Lik + Neon

If the glint of sunshine bouncing off the mirrored Perspex walls and three cats lounging on the counter don't instantly draw you in, then the stark white interior and ceiling installation of upturned milk bottles certainly will. With shelves piled with all kinds of seductive clutter from neon wallets and wristbands to framed illustrations and witty '5 second illustration' greetings cards, **Lik + Neon** places itself in a league of it's own. Fanzines by local artists and magazines celebrating people who look cool adorn one wall, with rare vinyl, cassette tapes, vintage Adidas, 'Tron' style jewellery and felt rings thrown in for good measure. No fashionable store in Shoreditch though would be complete without an eclectic selection of graphic sweatshirts and over-sized t-shirts, hailing Lik Neon as the gift shop for the 'Museum of Cool'. *PB*

MAP 1 Ref. 9

Lik + Neon
106 Sclater Street
Brick Lane E1 6HR
+44 (0)20 7729 4650
www.likneon.blogspot.com
Mon 12–7pm
Tue–Sat 11–7pm
Sun 11–6.30pm

Mendoza

Sixties inspired clothes shops come and go, usually because the novelty of dressing like an extra from Austin Powers wears off fairly quickly. **Mendoza** however is not about velvet and white knee high boots. Here you will find a serious menswear shop for those with a penchant for tailoring and classic Sixties Mod style. The Mod look was favoured by working class youths in the 1960's and encapsulated a very specific style of dress. Owner Leroy, a long established Mod himself realised a gap in the market for a look that despite the choice these days is hard to come by. Here you can walk in and walk out with an entirely new image. Mendoza will sort you out from head to toe, from Chelsea boots to tailored slacks in various pin stripes, tweed and chequered patterns not to mention the selection of short blouson style zipper jackets, turtle necks and ex-army parkas. *PB*

MAP 1 Ref. 8
Mendoza
158 Brick Lane
Brick Lane E1 6RU
+44 (0)20 7377 5263
www.mendozamenswear.com
Mon–Sun 12–6pm

My Robot Friends

The name '**My Robot Friends**' gives it away, this store sells toy robots. Lots of them. It's more of an art installation than a shop really, unless of course you're out to buy a robot. It depends which one though as I overhear the owner, John telling a customer "I'm going to hold onto that one unless someone makes me an offer I can't refuse". He's always loved robots, he used to collect them as a kid and now many of them are true rarities. It's not just robots mind you, among the nostalgia you will find Japanese Tengu masks and Dia de Muertos trinkets. There's plenty of things to make you smile – pretty fabric toys made by gypsies in Kashmir and all kinds of kitsch religious jewellery. John likes to think of his shop as a place to rediscover things you liked as a child. "It's about cool stuff" he says, "I have my fans!". *PB*

MAP 1 Ref. 11

My Robot Friends
20 Cheshire Street
Brick Lane E2 6EH
+44 (0)7974 155 031
www.myrobotfriends.co.uk
Thu–Sun 12–6pm

Number Six

"We want to sell clothes that people will be wearing in 10 years". In a time where everything is disposable this is a nice sentiment. Stockists of some exceptionally well crafted men's apparel including Barbour, Libertine Libertine and Sebago, **Number Six** is at the forefront of menswear stores. Here you can buy everything from the toes up - shoes, socks, coats, hats, bags and sunglasses and all in the best brands. The store itself is a stylish fit with industrial pipes, 70's furniture, antique cabinets, stag's antlers and framed butterflies – a nod to the ever fashionable Victoriana of East London. It's the bright green astro-turf effect floor, which sets this menswear store apart from the rest though. A slight afterthought, as the floor was apparently in a bit of state, it's nothing short of genius creating the perfect environment for men where it might almost be like shopping on a football pitch. *PB*

MAP 1 Ref. 7
Number Six
6 Dray Walk
91–95 Brick Lane
Brick Lane E1 6QL
+44 (0)20 7392 9686
www.numbersixlondon.com
Tue–Fri 10.30–6.30pm
Sat–Sun 11–6.30pm

Jessie Chorley & Buddug - the shop

Push pass the woollen slip of large stitches that masquerades as a door sign and enter a rose-scented fairytale of textile and text, matter and madness. Walls are papered with fading stories, china teacup candles waft sweet warmth and handmade cards and corsages clutter every surface. **Jessie & Buddug** are artschool friends who employ their Welsh language and heritage of romantic tradition to seductive effect in work that embraces theatrical installations such as Selfridges' Alice in Wonder Room, their individual fine art practices and all the offerings in this eponymous shop: handmade albums for your photos and ephemera, customised vintage linen, lace and wool garments, enamelled jewellery engraved with favourite phrases and the loveliest Lovespoons, crafted from combinations of wood, metal and fabric. Choose their gift tokens or commission a piece from the bespoke wedding range to make someone feel very special. *GT*

MAP 4 Ref. 42
Jessie Chorley & Buddug
158a Columbia Road
E2 7RG
+44 (0)7704708577
+44 (0)7708921550
www.jessiechorley.com
www.buddug.com
Tue–Fri (By appointment)
Sat 12–5pm Sun 9–4pm

L'Orangerie

As with a walk through botanical gardens, navigating a path round **L'Orangerie** requires some limber moves. Arranged along tall tables interposed with bay trees is a heady, clinking menagerie of colour, form and overhanging jewellery. Brush past fellow pickers in the slinky aisles and try not to catch your hair on a butterfly brooch or leafy earrings. It's an approach to selling that will infuriate or intoxicate. Those who surrender easily to the resinous slick of a bauble, clip or ring will appreciate the affordable prices and eccentric aesthetic. The overwhelmed should escape to the spacious calm of the lower level. Here the reward is a choice of kilim textiles, Panamas and floppy-brimmed sunhats à la Francoise Gilot, whose look encapsulates the style of L'Orangerie. *GT*

MAP 4 Ref. 43
L' Orangerie
162 Columbia Road
E2 7RG
+44 (0)7525 004300
Sat 10–5pm
Sun 8.30–5.30pm

Marcos and Trump

West End girls with East End lives could do worse than refresh their wardrobe at **Marcos and Trump**, the boutique with an eye on both worlds. The mission statement is to provide a style that will endure both seasonal change and financial fluctuation as well as the crosstown flow of a London life. How to achieve this? With a mainstay of labels such as Peopletree, Full Circle and Darling, alongside Melissa for shoes and occasional others who provide a nod to the more fleeting phases of fashion. There's a strong evening and partywear bias which allows for the very ingenious range of Fashion First Aid accessories, designed to deal with boobs that just won't sit up, lie flat, or do whatever it is exactly THAT dress requires of them. Ultimately, it's a girls world. *GT*

MAP 4 Ref. 41

Marcos and Trump
146 Columbia Road
E2 7RG
+44 (0)20 7739 9008
www.marcosandtrump.com
Thu–Fri 12–6pm
Sat 11–6pm Sun 9–4pm

-10%

*Discount**

MiLagros

This is the shop that vies with the market for colour, and comes out on top. As sure as the bees fly to the flowers outside many will find themselves drawn to the florid interior of this Mexican microcosm. Stunningly incongruous, **Milagros** has everything you wanted to buy on holiday but weren't sure would survive the plane journey home. Jet-lagged customers aren't unknown. Saints, skeletons, virgins and wrestlers all make an appearance alongside the votive paintings, handcrafted paper cuts and bubbly recycled glassware. The latest addition is a range of baskets, immaculately hand-woven from galvanised wire and polythene. They come in a variety of colours and four standard forms but, as with the ceramic tiles, can be commissioned in any other size or colour, such is the value of an independent outlet that has a personal relationship with all its suppliers. *GT*

MAP 4 Ref. 39

Milagros
61 Columbia Road
E2 7RG
+44 (0)20 7613 0876
www.milagros.co.uk
Mon–Sat (By appointment)
Sun 9–4pm

StartSpace

Is it a gallery or a café? No, it's a café and a coffee bar. A gallery sandwich? Oh, I don't know. Whatever. **StartSpace** has not one, but two coffee outlets with a gallery space in between, and it's all extremely pleasant. Pick up a latte from the skinniest slip of a stand, a mere doorway wide, then take a wander through the grey-washed interior to reflect on the paintings. Figurative and abstract work, from contemporary mid-career artists, is the staple. There's usually a group show, occasionally some sculpture and always a few select pieces of applied art. The contrast with the frenzy of the market couldn't be more marked and it's a truly refreshing and relaxed environment in which to appreciate artwork. By the time you reach the veranda with its kitchen café your heart rate should have dropped a few beats and it'll be time for another coffee. *GT*

MAP 4 Ref. 40
StartSpace
150 Columbia Road
E2 7RG
+44 (0)20 7729 0522
www.startspace.co.uk
Sat 12–6pm
Sun 8–3pm

Suck & Chew

Not a place for the diabetically inclined, **Suck & Chew** even smells dangerous. The sugared air taunts with essences of banana, kola, aniseed and custard. If you can't remember the last time you had a pink flying saucer stuck to the roof of your mouth, your tongue turned evil with a Black Jack or your jaw locked down with a Fruit Salad then make haste to Suck and Chew, the shop that time forgot. All the old favourites are here and the jars are just as big as ever. An irreverent humour flavours the décor and the imaginative employment of original coronation mugs and technicolor vintage tins for packaging guarantees some rare and very good value gifts. Can't make it to the shop? Buy online. Can't bear to leave? Invite them to pop-up at your office party, birthday or wedding. Willy Wonka, eat your heart out! *GT*

MAP 4 Ref. 37
Suck & Chew
130 Columbia Road
E2 7RG
+44 (0)20 8983 3504
www.suckandchew.co.uk
Thu–Fri 12–6pm
Sat 12–5pm
Sun 9–4.30pm

Supernice

Decals rule the day in this showroom of sticky wall style. If you're the type to bore quickly or just crave the satisfaction of being able to personalise your living space then **Supernice** is for you. Collaborations with a number of designers and illustrators have brought about a range of removable wall art that features flora and fauna, computer games, abstract artwork and some very smart trompe l'oeil furniture. The big-selling brand is Blik, this being their main outlet in Europe, every surface is used to great effect to display the elements which vary from cute to cool. The alphabet comes in decals, plywood and stoneware tiles and Supernice also stocks great graphics from Thomas Paul, Inke and Threadless. If you can't get to the shop, check the website which has some nifty display functions. *GT*

MAP 4 Ref. 36
Supernice
106 Columbia Road
E2 7RG
+44 (0)20 7613 3890
www.supernice.co.uk
Mon–Fri (By appointment)
Sat 1–6pm
Sun 9.30–3.30pm

The Powder Room

Turn your green fingers pink with pleasure. By popular demand **The Powder Room**, in all its candy-striped glory, has landed safely in the East End. These former flying doctors of the beauty world are now firmly established as a fixed entity on Columbia Road, albeit at weekends only for the time being. All you have to decide is how much time-out you can take in this palace of pampering. Nail treatments are 15, 30 or 40 minutes in duration and with prices starting at £15 you'll still have change for flowers. Make-up, new lashes or the latest 'Up Do' can be administered pretty swiftly too. Prices include tea and biscuits which make it a very affordable break from a breathless weekend. But if glamour is your weekday vice, don't forget the Soho branch – open Monday to Saturday. *GT*

MAP 4 Ref. 38
The Powder Room
136 Columbia Road
E2 7RG
+44 (0)844 879 4928
www.thepowderpuffgirls.com
Sat 12–6pm
Sun 10–4pm

Vintage Heaven

'I say, what's this?' Here among the 1953 Schoolfriend Annual, the wooden badminton racquet that weighs like concrete and the battered tartan Thermos is, well, everything but Grandma's kitchen sink. This one-woman collection, gathered over a lifetime's obsession with house sales, fetes and car boots really is vintage heaven. She did it so you don't have to. Just make sure you get here before it sells out – the Americans have been bulk-buying. Cross-stitch scenes of The Last Supper and kitsch landscapes with pink skies are winners, as are the acres of textiles, tea sets and bone-handled cutlery. The piles of publications feature worthy wartime recipes, knitting patterns plus a whole lot of horticulture. And the lastword n teatime must be **Vintage Heaven**'s Cakehole café, a wholly retro delight.
GT

MAP 4 Ref. 35
Vintage Heaven
82 Columbia Road
E2 7QB
+44 (0)1277 215968
www.vintageheaven.co.uk
Mon–Thu (By appointment)
Fri 12–5pm
Sat 12–6pm
Sun 8.30–5.30pm

Wawa

Wawa is a bright and tactile showroom, full of colour, is the workspace of bespoke furniture maker Richard Ward. Specialising in seating, his signature Soho Two sofa is a diminutive and elegant two-seater and the most recent design, Bay, was devised to fit the 'bay window' so typical of London homes. As with all his pieces, proportions can be modified to fit any space: depth, height and length are all variable, even the profile of the cushions attracts his meticulous attention to detail. In a charming acknowledgment, new commissions are often named for the client – thus Yasmin, Oscar and Dorothee, each with its own distinctive character. The shop sells other homewares, mostly by UK designers but it's worth visiting for the extensive fabric department alone, with its strong emphasis on texture and featuring the likes of Kenzo, Lelievre and Sahco among other classic names. *GT*

MAP 4 Ref. 44
Wawa
1 Ezra Street
E2 7RH
+44 (0)20 7729 6768
www.wawa.co.uk
Weekdays (By appointment)
Sun 10–2.30pm

Towner & Hoxton

Café. Hackney Central

Artists Adam Towner & Johnny Hoxton have taken the opportunity offered to them by a supportive landlord to create a gallery and tea room in Well Street, Hackney. Unfortunately this is an exception it would seem, as the major landlord in Well street seeks to extract more money by doubling rents to its shopkeepers. This is hardly justified In a street that has seen a lot of neglect. It is time large landlords like this contributed more to the upkeep of neighborhoods. There used to be eleven butchers, seven greengrocers and a couple of fish stalls here. All in the street where it all began for Tesco, it was here that barrowboy Jack Cohen had his pitch in 1919, going on to build the Tesco empire. He later came back to put a branch at the top of the street in 1970, soon seeing off the street market with the last fruit and veg stall giving up last year, now just one pitch remains. Good luck to Adam and Johnny and check there site for events and happenings.

Towner & Hoxton
Gallery and Tea
233 Well Street
E9 6RG
www.townerandhoxton.com
Sat & Sun 12–7pm

Artwords Bookshop

Rueing the demise of Borders and suffering cold turkey for your fashion magazine fix? **Artwords** can ease your pain. Seven days a week, Artwords offers the full extended qwerty of contemporaryvisualculture with thwacking great style mags making up a serious chunk of their selection. True there's no coffee-shop but with so many lining the street outside only the meanest would moan. Hackney is said to have the greatest concentration of artists in Europe and Broadway Market is surely an artery from the heart of this artistic community. Galleries, studios and workshops abound. To eavesdrop the in-shop conversations is to understand how the publications here reflect the knowledge base of the area. There's much to be found in this collection that isn't at Amazon but if your desire is arcane beyond their considerable ken, any omission can be ordered for you. You need never leave Hackney again. *GT*

MAP 5 Ref. 48
Artwords Bookshop
20–22 Broadway Market
E8 4QJ
+44 (0)20 7923 7507
www.artwords.co.uk
Mon–Fri 10.30–6.30pm
Sat 10–6pm
Sun 10.30–7pm

Black Truffle

Mary Poppins would find much to approve of in **Black Truffle**. And if you weren't practically perfectly shod before, you too will have no excuse once you've found this place. Run by a shoemaker, in tandem with an international school of shoemaking, there's no question of anything being less than top quality. From lace-up boots through Oxfords and brogues to Mary-Janes, peep-toes, espadrilles and pumps; for the discerning customer they've got it covered. Neither run-of-the-mill nor faddish there's a distinct brand aesthetic that's gently quirky, played out in the finest leather and cloth, fancy uppers stitched down firmly to quality soles. With so much attention to detail on the main event you could forgive a slacking in the sidelines, but no, here you'll find smocks and shirts, accessories and jewellery, all meeting the same criteria. The final flourish is the oddest gift shelf. I'll let you discover. *GT*

MAP 5 Ref. 46

Black Truffle
4 Broadway Market
E8 4PH
+44 (0)20 7923 9450
www.blacktruffle.com
Tue-Fri 11–6pm
Sat 10–6pm
Sun 12–6pm

The Broadway Bookshop

As the girl beside me, browsing with her friend pointed out, "This is how bookshops should be arranged, it makes so much sense". Absolutely. In fact, I was so involved in my journey of perusal that I'd long stopped analysing the unusual thematic taxonomy at **The Broadway Bookshop**. Mired in the nature studies section where William Burroughs' The Cat Inside rubs jackets with Food for Free, the 1970s classic by Richard Mabey, my reverie was enhanced by the comforting mustiness emanating from the third and lowest level of this diminutive store. With the air of a library, here you'll find the vintage treasures: rare charity shop acquisitions, tomes that have arrived by donation and other long-loved volumes. It's not all nostalgic though. Upstairs the stock is as bang up to date as at any online outlet with the added value of a warm and knowledgeable personal service. *GT*

MAP 5 Ref. 47
The Broadway Bookshop
6 Broadway Market
E8 4QJ
+44 (0)20 7241 1626
www.broadwaybookshophackney.co.u
Tue–Sat 10–6pm
Sun 11–5pm

Fabrications

According to my dictionary a 'fabrication' is constructed or manufactured from prepared components. **Fabrications** on Broadway Market is woven of the strands, shop, studio and workshop classroom. It's good to know this before you arrive. You might otherwise wonder what exactly it is that you've encountered – this colourful cube being little more than a shop-front for a multitude of activities focused on sustainability. Cocooned in haberdashery, British wools, publications on knitting and sewing, eco home-wares, gifts and some well-worth-a-rummage off-cuts bins, regular craft classes in all manner of textile techniques take place in the main space. Downstairs is the studio. Here 'Up-cycling' dominates all practice, from proprietor Barley Massey's textile design business, to the Remember Me service whereby your long-loved but aged garment, saggy and loose at the seams, can be commissioned for revival as a quilt, artwork or other textile worth treasuring for yet another lifetime. *GT*

MAP 5 Ref. 50

Fabrications
7 Broadway Market
E8 4PH
+44 (0)20 7275 8043
www.fabrications1.co.uk
Tue–Fri 12–5pm
Sat 10–5.30pm
Sun: workshops

*Free loyalty card stamp**

Fin & Flounder

Narrow as a ship's galley, **Fin & Flounder** is replete with the essentials for your fish dinner, the back wall lined with condiments and herbs, the counter bearing baskets of lemons. Newly licenced, they now feature a sensibly slim selection of predominantly Italian wines. Anxieties can be left at the door as the management supply fish only from Marine Stewardship Council preferred sources. Where the criteria can't be met they simply won't stock an item, preferring instead to market 'bycatch', the often disregarded by-product of a fishing excursion. This makes for a far more interesting shopping experience than at the supermarket where the packets are the same shape every day. Under its blue awning, the sluiced and tiled interior sings of the sea and fishmongers of a bygone age. These nostalgic notes are no accident as the team delivers a proper service and can advise on preparation and recipes. *GT*

MAP 5 Ref. 53
Fin & Flounder
71 Broadway Market
E8 4PH
+44 (0)7838 018 395
www.finandflounder.com
Tue-–Fri 10–6.30
Sat 9–5pm
Sun 11–4pm

l'eau à La Bouche

Named for the Gainsbourg song, welcome to 'mouth-watering' the café. The food and the tunes here are global in their reach, although, like the sausages in the deli, with a distinct North African flavour. This is the joint that feeds the food stars, catering recently for Nigel Slater and his Simple Suppers team, so it's worth staying for more than just a coffee. Fresh produce is mostly sourced locally or at least from within Europe, never air-freighted and served seasonally. The deli and grocery shelves proffer British basics alongside continental goodies and the wine racks are the pride of the proprietor. Since the move from smaller premises along the way **l'eau à La Bouche** has grown its clientele to fill the bigger space, and then some. Even on a grey day there's enough of a cosmopolitan gaggle at the tables outside to shame any Parisian equivalent. *GT*

MAP 5 Ref. 51
l'eau à La Bouche
35-37 Broadway Market
E8 4PH
+44 (0)20 7923 0600
www.labouche.co.uk
Mon–Fri 8.30–7pm
Sat 8.30–5pm
Sun 9.30–5pm

The Last Tuesday Society

A bit of fluffy taxidermy, in the cheery light of day, can sure pull on the purse strings. Throw in a birthday poo card, a few meteorite shards and Susanna's front-bottom, forever foxy in formaldehyde (yours for £125) and you'll definitely win the prize for best present. However, one might want to think twice before releasing anything from the Pandora's box that is the creepy canal-side cellar of **The Last Tuesday Society**. Here below the shop and art gallery lie the motley and the monstrous, things of fact and fiction and the "doctored back end of a deer". Hours may be lost in this underworld of provocation where Gary Glitter, Enid Blyton and Mr. Robertson's golliwogs seem entirely at home amongst the relics in this, the only place ever known to promote the purchase of a fur jacket with the assurance that it's the skin of a 'long-dead' animal. *GT*

MAP 5 Ref. 54

The Last Tuesday Society
11 Mare Street
E8 8RP
+44 (0)20 7998 3617
www.thelasttuesdaysociety.org
Wed–Sun 12–7pm

Lock 7

Pragmatically positioned on what must be London's most biked thoroughfare, is the lovely, so lofty **Lock 7**. With its high ceilings, raw concrete floor and Scandi style you might just want to move in. This pit stop of repair and sustenance is like no other and the dominant feature, it has to be said, is girls. Run by girls and mostly staffed by girls, its great popularity can be attributed to the good nature, sound advice and genuine commitment to bike health of the team. These local business ingénues who started up with nothing more than a desire to keep good bicycles off the scrap pile are now at the helm of a thriving enterprise that sells great coffee, food to beat any dedicated outlet, every part and accessory you could possibly need - and the multi-coloured versions you probably don't – with quick turnaround services at entirely reasonable prices. *GT*

MAP 5 Ref. 45

Lock 7
129 Pritchards Road
Broadway Market E2 9AP
+44 (0)20 7739 3042
www.lock-7.com
Tue–Sat 8–6pm
Sun 10–6pm

Our Patterned Hand

Our patterned hand might better be called unpatterned so little is repeated at this hip haberdasher. Established by a deserter from the fashion industry, jaded with the increasing standardisation so prevalent in popular fashion, most items are the antithesis of the mass-produced. Aside from the full extent of sewing supplies there's a rainbow of dyes and fabric paints and a selection of fabrics to rival any West End specialist.
The stock comprises limited edition digital prints from Italy, one-off lengths of kimono fabric exquisitely hand-worked and prints from local designers, all in natural fibres. Buttons are made of bone, paper and plant fibres – no plastic – and if you don't quite know what to do with all this wonderful stuff then you'll be welcome in the workshop downstairs where someone is on hand to help with your tailoring or customising project. *GT*

MAP 5 Ref. 52
Our Patterned Hand
49 Broadway Market
E8 4RE
+44 (0)20 7812 9912
www.patternedhand.co.uk
Tue–Fri 10–6pm
Sat 10–5pm Sun 12–5pm

Halfway between the grasses of London Fields and the wildflowers of the Regent's canal flourishes a variety of colour and foliage that isn't so dissimilar. Culled from across the British isles – gardens commercial and private – it's to be found at **Rebel Rebel**, the standalone flower shop that has said a firm 'no' to the standardised arrangements required by the international delivery folk and created a style that regularly attracts commissions from TV companies, fashion houses and arts institutions. Fortunately this high profile activity hasn't stopped them continuing to offer the simplest pleasures to the casual passer-by. Bestsellers are humble cornflowers, at three quid a bunch. Other favourites being dahlias, sweetpeas, delphiniums and jasmine. Anything can be bought as a single stem and frequent visits will reward the enthusiast as the seasons are marked by an ever-changing stock that is subject to the wanderings of the British climate. *GT*

MAP 5 Ref. 49

Rebel Rebel
5 Broadway Market
E8 4PH
+44 (0)20 7254 4487
www.rebelrebel.co.uk
Tue–Fri 10–6pm
Sat 9–5pm

Bottle Apostle

It's all here, plus beer. Owner Andrew spotted a yawning chasm in the market and filled it with wines from around the world. Smaller boutique producers are strongly featured and on any visit you can taste up to 32 wines from the Enomatic machine. **Bottle Apostle** will track your purchases for you, enabling you to repeat your favourites and allowing them to propose new ones, of which they have roughly 15 per week. Within a year of opening they have acquired a loyal clientele perhaps seduced by the sociability of their weekly events: nights of German wines served with Vietnamese flavours from neighbouring Namo or suggestions for fish with a lesson in prep from the local fishmonger. It's hard in this most gentle patch of London to escape the village shop vibe and these blow-ins are no exception. The team are welcoming, unpretentious and friendly, their enthusiasm engaging. *GT*

MAP 5 Ref. 56
Bottle Apostle
95 Lauriston Road
Victoria Village E9 7MJ
+44 (0)20 8985 1549
www.bottleapostle.com
Tue–Fri 12–9pm
Sat 10–8pm
Sun 10–6pm

Branch on the park

The traditional hierarchies of value are laid to waste in the jewellery of Julia Cook. All stones are equal in the eyes of this designer and all merit the same careful consideration in their presentation. Created at her bench in his lovely shop-studio, pieces incorporate the full spectrum of precious and semi-precious stones, bound in gold and silver, with motifs from nature as recurrent themes. She works to commission and the items on display are ideal starting points for a bespoke process that will culminate in something entirely unique. More accessible items by her can by enjoyed for as little as £25 or less for those of other British designers such as Galibardy, frillybylily, Samantha Salmons and Stolen Thunder whose hand-drawn graphics wrought in wood and acrylic stand out. **Branch on the park** is a browser's delight with portraits, paintings and a collection of crystals and fossils sure to fascinate young visitors. *GT*

MAP 5 Ref. 61
Branch on the park
227 Victoria Park Road
Victoria Village E9 7HD
+44 (0)20 8533 7977
www.branchonthepark.co.uk
Wed–Sat 10–6pm
Sun 11–5pm

Haus

Haus is a stately parkside emporium where you'll find a sharp edit of the most stylish international design with British manufacture taking pride of place. Underpinned by heavyweights B&B Italia, Edra and Marimekko the bias favours less widely represented companies such as Lightyears (who brought you the Caravaggio lamp), Swedese and Hackney's hottest Decode, Uniformwares and Frank. Owner Andrew Tye has been working out of Hackney for over 15 years designing and making furniture under his own name. The relationships that have been forged in that time explain why you'll often find prototypes from other designers here before they hit the mainstream, making visits so rewarding. And it's hard to leave empty-handed when the smaller gift size items include such ingenious solutions as universal lids to transform old jam jars into cutting edge condiment vessels. Bespoke pieces can always be commissioned or sourced by Andrew – so do ask! *GT*

MAP 5 Ref. 55

Haus
39 Morpeth Road
Victoria Village E9 7LD
+44 (0)20 7536 9291
www.hauslondon.com
Sat 11–6pm
Sun 11–4pm

*Offer ends 1st Nov 2011 **

Loafing

You couldn't find a better place to loaf than **Loafing**. Where, gratifyingly, you can also buy a loaf: fresh bread arrives daily from St. John's and Flour Power. Coffee is the best on the block, as voted by the Victoria Park Traders' Association last year and is served in the prettiest china you'll have sipped from in a long time. This café is a whole wonderful world away from what we've become accustomed to on the high street. The décor is alluring, owing to its previous incarnation as an antiques shop and it hasn't lost a crumb of style since. If you can drag yourself away from the sweetest piles of patisserie out front, be sure to make time for a lunchtime sarnie in the garden – Ginger Pig ham and chutney perhaps – or bag an armchair by the window for an afternoon Earl Grey with a friend. *GT*

MAP 5 Ref. 57

Loafing
79 Lauriston Road
Victoria Village E9 7MJ
+44 (0)20 8986 0777
www.loafing.co.uk
Mon–Fri 7.30–6pm
Sat 8–6pm
Sun 9–6pm

The Residence

A renowned commentator of the London art scene described **The Residence** as "the place to be seen… the Guggenheim of the East End". Ever-evolving it now boasts its own guest suite for hire: an extrapolation of the enduring residential theme – home as gallery – as explored in previous incarnations at other venues. Arch directrice Ingrid Z has been curating shows since her own art school days in Canada and has her finger on the pulsing flow. If you fancy edging so close to bleeding, this is where it's at. She believes artists represent the gallery not the other way round and at The Residence she facilitates a lively roster of them: emerging and established. Prices for the freshest of 21st Century Fine Art are on a scale of affordable to serious. Underestimate at your peril. *GT*

MAP 5 Ref. 62
The Residence
229 Victoria Park Road
Victoria Village E9 7HD
+44 (0)20 8985 0321
www.residence-gallery.com
Wed–Sat 11–6pm
Sun 12–5pm

Sublime

Sublime's success is built on long-standing attention to its customers needs. Starting out over a decade ago as little more than a gift shop it's been a natural evolution to its current one-stop-shop position for presents and party dresses as well as casuals for the style-savvy but time-poor mums of the East. In the cavernous vintage section downstairs however, this boutique shows its heart. A perusal uncovers not just well-chosen retro garments, shoes and accessories but some brand spanking new garb, often still bearing original tags, no doubt via way of a shoot with one of the many stylists who live nearby. There are pieces for all ages, reflecting the influence of both staff and customers. Back upstairs, labels such as ethical Peopletree and local designers emilyandfin fit well with the holistic sense of this outlet whose focus is firmly on enduring style rather than disposable fashion. A newer Clerkenwell branch continues the theme. *GT*

MAP 5 Ref. 60
Sublime
225 Victoria Park Road
Victoria Village E9 7HD
+44 (0)20 8986 7243
www.sublimeshop.co.uk
Mon–Fri 10–6pm
Sat 9–7pm
Sun 11–5pm

The Toybox

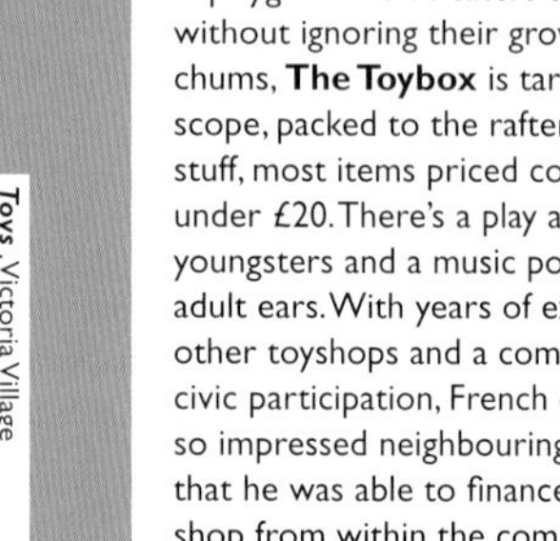

A playground that caters to children without ignoring their grown-up chums, **The Toybox** is tardis-like in its scope, packed to the rafters with fun stuff, most items priced comfortably under £20. There's a play area for youngsters and a music policy to cheer adult ears. With years of experience in other toyshops and a commitment to civic participation, French owner Loic so impressed neighbouring businesses that he was able to finance the new shop from within the community. His tribute to the area is an array of imaginative and well-made games and toys dominated by the gorgeous French range Djeco whose crafty kits and removable sticker sets are deserved top-sellers alongside Sockette puppets (for long arms as much as little fingers) packed in amongst all the old favourites: board games, marbles, trainsets, puzzles, books and, as you might expect from a French proprietor, some particularly chic clothing. *GT*

MAP 5 Ref. 59
The Toybox
223 Victoria Park Road
Victoria Village E9 7HD
+44 (0)20 8533 2879
www.thetoyboxshop.co.uk
Mon–Sun 9–6pm

Victoria Park Books

There's something elevating about **Victoria Park Books**. It doesn't take long to notice. So unassuming, so calm. But more. Beyond the shop front, this children's bookshop is a messianic force, visiting schools and events, bringing authors and illustrators to the field, the aim not just to grow an east London community of readers who will value a book as much as the latest technological gadget but to water the seed of local literary talent. Rooted in a family heritage of bookselling there's an integrity that permeates every shelf. All books are personally recommended by the shop owners with their young family being the litmus for the children's choice. The ten percent or so of adult literature feels greater due to the breadth of stock and harmonious domesticity is supported by an abundance of choice through gardening, cookery and family health. *GT*

MAP 5 Ref. 58

Victoria Park Books
174 Victoria Park Road
Victoria Village E9 7HD
+44 (0)20 8986 1124
www.victoriaparkbooks.co.uk
Tue–Sun 10–5.30pm

Wilton Way

Wilton Way has found a way...

Behind Hackney Town Hall, above London Fields and to the right of Dalston lies **Wilton Way**. Hidden but now no longer over looked. Wilton Way has all the potential of any other successful street but hasn't been given the necessary creative vision and commitment to give it some focus. By up-cycling some key shops to new contemporary uses, David McHugh has shown what can be done with a street losing direction. Too often, potential in the high street has only a profit motive, this is too restrictive for many community streets and too often leads to the unimaginative, mass appeal, 'Dragons Den' (millionaire in a year) money making enterprises filling our streets and towns everywhere. What's needed is heartfelt commitment and the personal touch by people who live in the area and want to enjoy what they are giving to their customers and local community. Of course this wasn't done alone, H Brown formerly a shoe shop, was reborn (at least partly) as a shoe shop. 'The Otherside of the Pillow' selling Deadstock and retro curios of every kind. While David and Dominik run the Wilton Way Café, a former electrical shop serving great coffee, food and a regular radio show. While Julia Royse has 'reassigned' the Post Office as a gallery and coming soon are the Fish & Chippy with a difference and a new hairdresser. Also check out Violet café (cup cakes) and pubs The Spurstowe and Prince George. Wilton Way has found a way.

The Other Side of the Pillow 61 Wilton Way E8 / www.theothersideofthepillow.blogspot.com

Posted 67 Wilton Way E8 / www.postedprojects.co.uk

Violet 47 Wilton Way E8 / www.violetcakes.com

Wilton Way Café 63 Wilton Way E8 / www.londonfieldsradio.com

MAP
1
E1/E2
Shoreditch MAP 2
The Book Club
Great Eastern St.
Holywell Ln
Rich Mix
Bethnal Green
Beigle Bake
Brick Lane
Sclater St
Cheshire St
SHOREDITCH
Eastside Books
Lounge Bohemia
Commercial Tavern
Buxton S
21 mins. walk
SPITALFIELDS
Rough Trade
Story
Old Truman Brewery
1,001
Folgate St
Spital Sq
Lamb St
The Golden Heart
Rosa's
Nude
Hanbury St
Spitalfields Market
Fournier St
Pride of Spitalfields
Brushfield St
Market Coffee House
Ten Bells
Commercial St.
Heneag
Fashion St
Chicksa
Artillery Ln
Bishopsgate
8,11,23,26,35,48,133,149,214
BUS
The Bell
Bell Ln
LIVERPOOL STREET
Cobb St
WHITECHAPEL
23
22
20
19
18
16
14
13
12
11
10
9
8
7
6
5
4
3
2
1

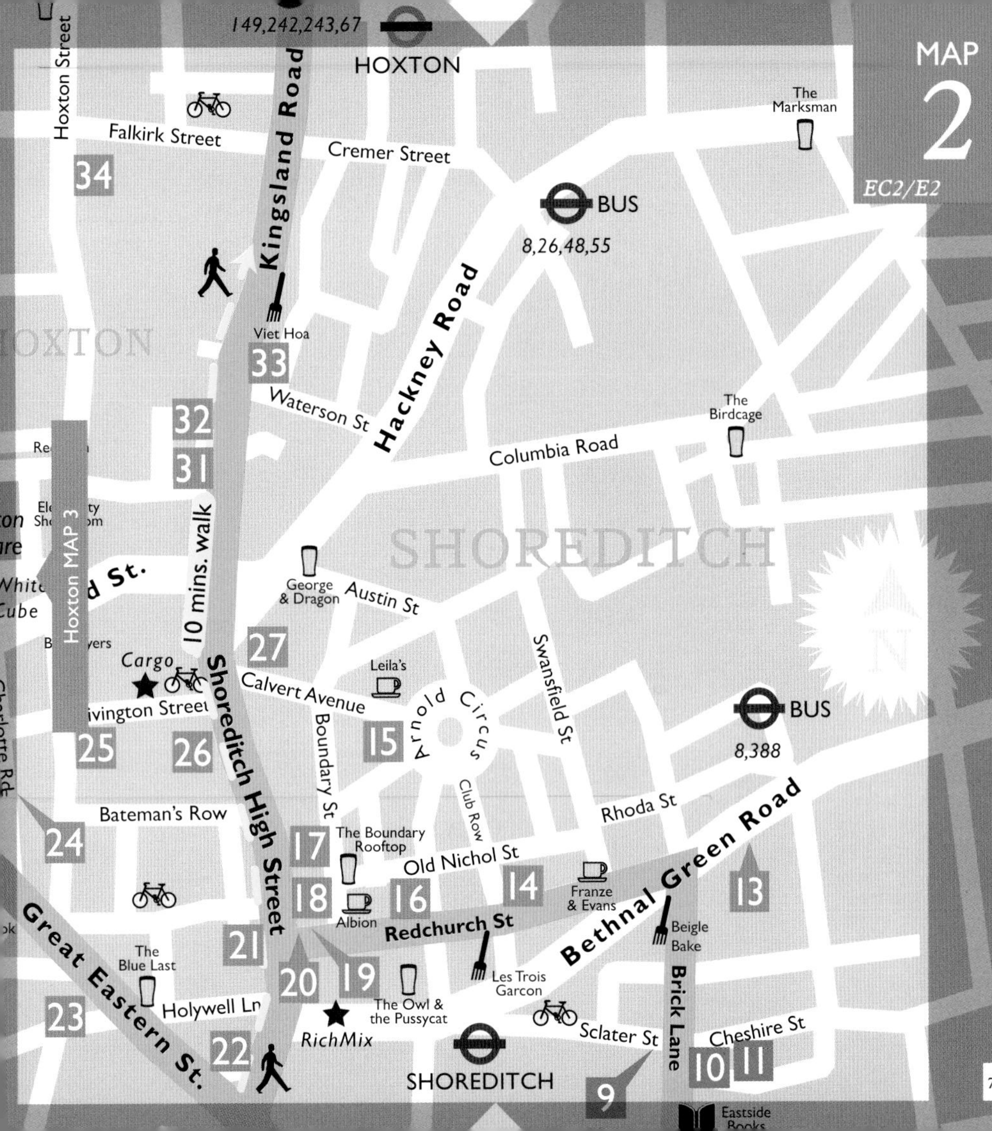
MAP
2
EC2/E2
HOXTON
149,242,243,67
Hoxton Street
Falkirk Street
Cremer Street
Kingsland Road
The Marksman
BUS
8,26,48,55
Hackney Road
Viet Hoa
33
34
Waterson St
32
31
The Birdcage
Columbia Road
10 mins. walk
Hoxton MAP 3
SHOREDITCH
George & Dragon
Austin St
27
Cargo
Shoreditch High Street
Calvert Avenue
Leila's
Arnold Circus
Swansfield St
Boundary St
15
BUS
8,388
25
26
Club Row
Rhoda St
Bateman's Row
24
17
The Boundary Rooftop
Old Nichol St
14
Bethnal Green Road
13
18
16
Franze & Evans
Albion
Redchurch St
Beigle Bake
21
Great Eastern St.
The Blue Last
20
19
Les Trois Garcon
Brick Lane
23
Holywell Ln
The Owl & the Pussycat
Sclater St
Cheshire St
RichMix
22
SHOREDITCH
10
11
9
Eastside Books

MAP
3
N1/EC2
White Hart
BUS
149,242,243,67
HOXTON
Hoxton Street
Falkirk Street
Kingsland Rd
Cremer Street
34
8,26,48,
HOXTON
Viet Hoa
33
Hackney Rd
Waterson St
Pitfield Street
32
31
Ruby
Red Lion
Cinema
Columbi
Hoxton Bar & Kitchen
Hoxton Square
Electricity Showroom
28
SHOREDIT
30
Cycle Lab & Juice Bar
White Cube
Old St
George & Dragon
Austin St
29
The Reliance
Bricklayers
Cargo
27
Calvert Avenue
Leila's
Arnold Circus
OLD ST.
11 mins. walk
Shoreditch MAP 2
Shoreditch High St
Boundary St
15
BUS
55,135,243
Botega Prelibato
Rivington Grill
25
26
The Princess of Shoreditch
Bateman's Row
Club Row
The Griffin
24
17
The Boundary Rooftop
Old Nichol
The Book Club
18
16
Leonard St
Albion
Redchurch Stre
Tabernacle St
Paul St
23
21
The Blue Last
Luke St
20
19
The Owl & the Pussycat
Holywell Ln
Rich Mix
City Roa
22

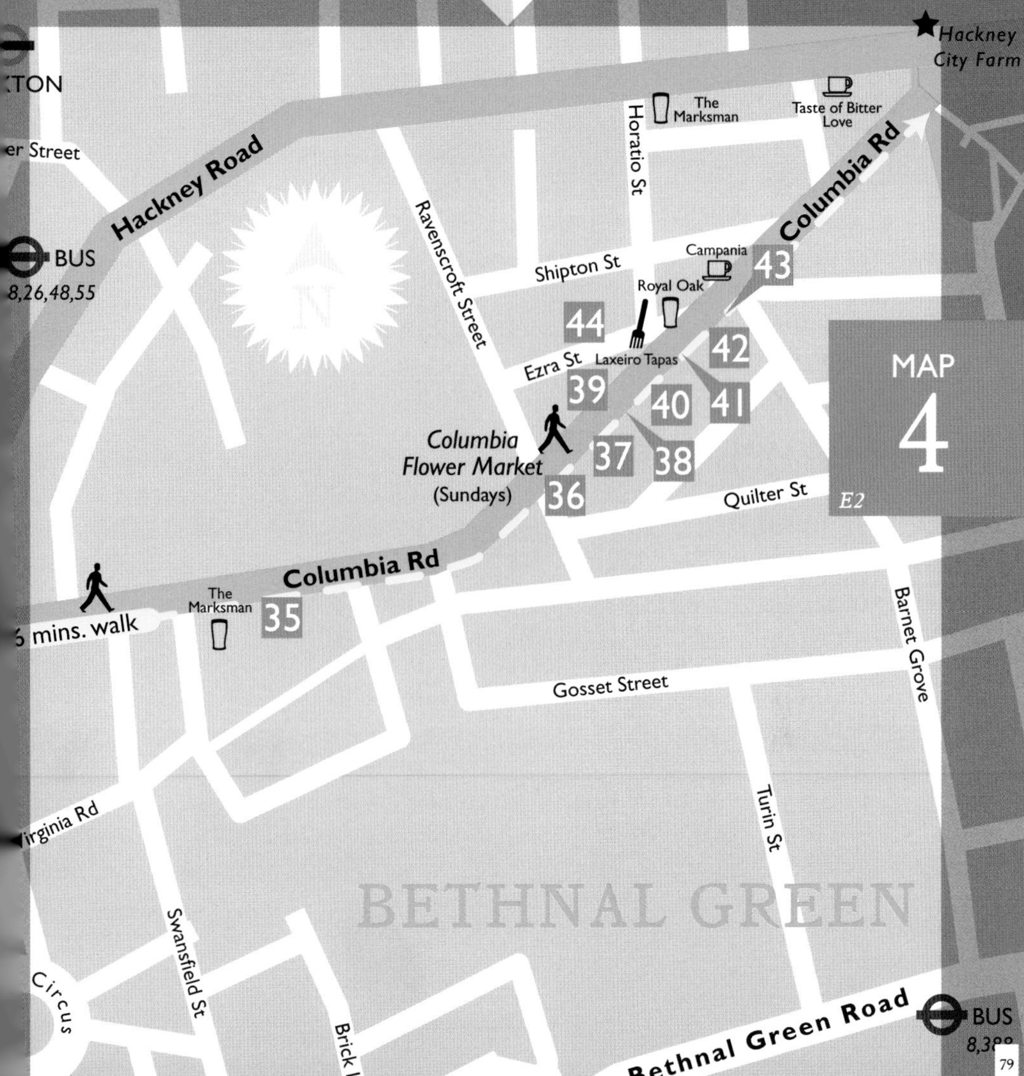
Hackney City Farm
The Marksman
Taste of Bitter Love
Horatio St
Hackney Road
Columbia Rd
BUS
8,26,48,55
Ravenscroft Street
Shipton St
Campania
Royal Oak
43
44
42
Ezra St
Laxeiro Tapas
39
40
41
MAP
4
E2
Columbia Flower Market (Sundays)
37
38
36
Quilter St
Columbia Rd
The Marksman
35
mins. walk
Barnet Grove
Gosset Street
Virginia Rd
Turin St
BETHNAL GREEN
Swansfield St
Circus
Brick Lane
Bethnal Green Road
BUS
Type

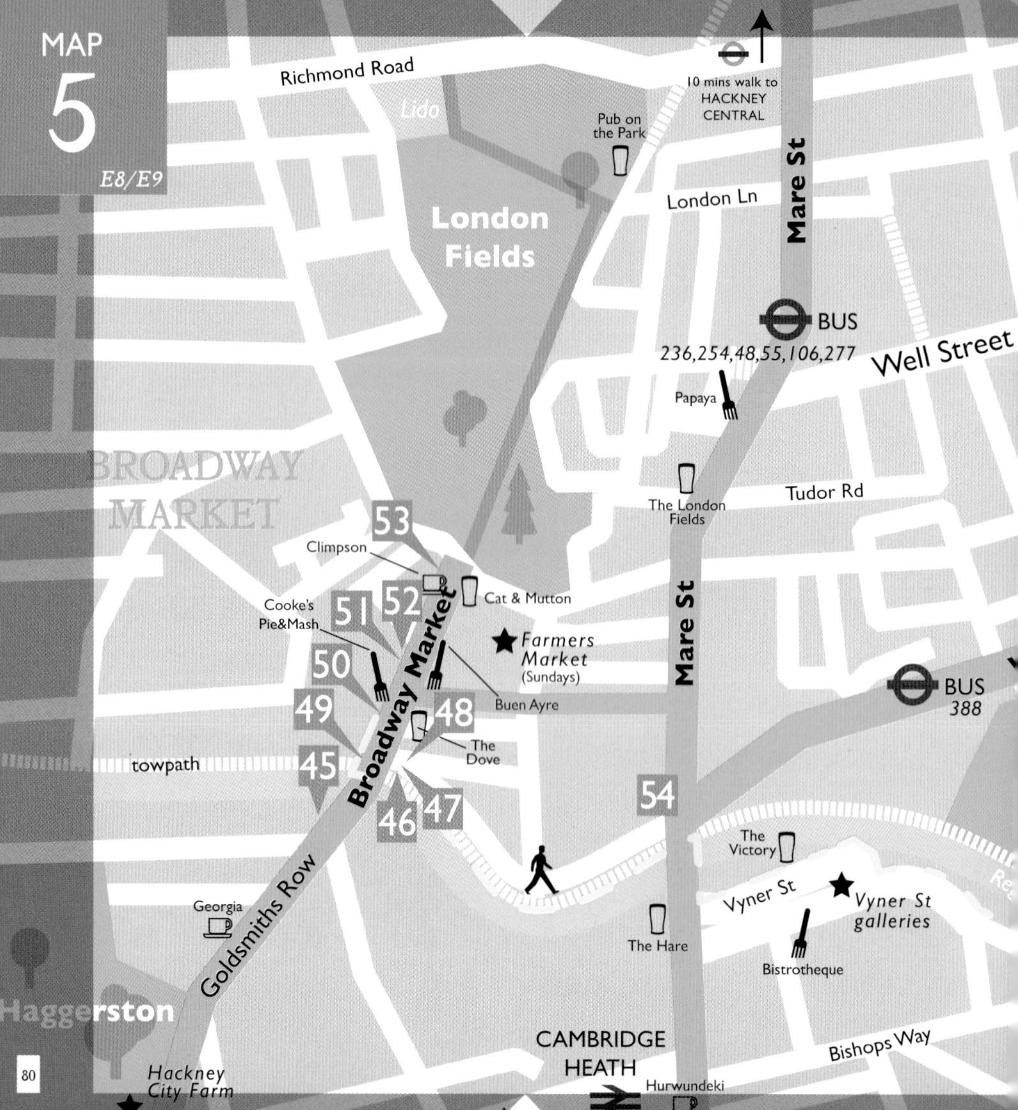
MAP
5
E8/E9
Richmond Road
Lido
10 mins walk to
HACKNEY
CENTRAL
Pub on
the Park
London Ln
Mare St
London
Fields
BUS
236,254,48,55,106,277
Well Street
Papaya
BROADWAY
MARKET
The London
Fields
Tudor Rd
53
Climpson
Cat & Mutton
52
51
Cooke's
Pie&Mash
Farmers
Market
(Sundays)
50
Broadway Market
Mare St
BUS
388
49
48
Buen Ayre
The
Dove
towpath
45
54
47
46
The
Victory
Vyner St
Vyner St
galleries
Georgia
Goldsmiths Row
The Hare
Bistrotheque
Haggerston
CAMBRIDGE
HEATH
Bishops Way
Hackney
City Farm
Hurwundeki

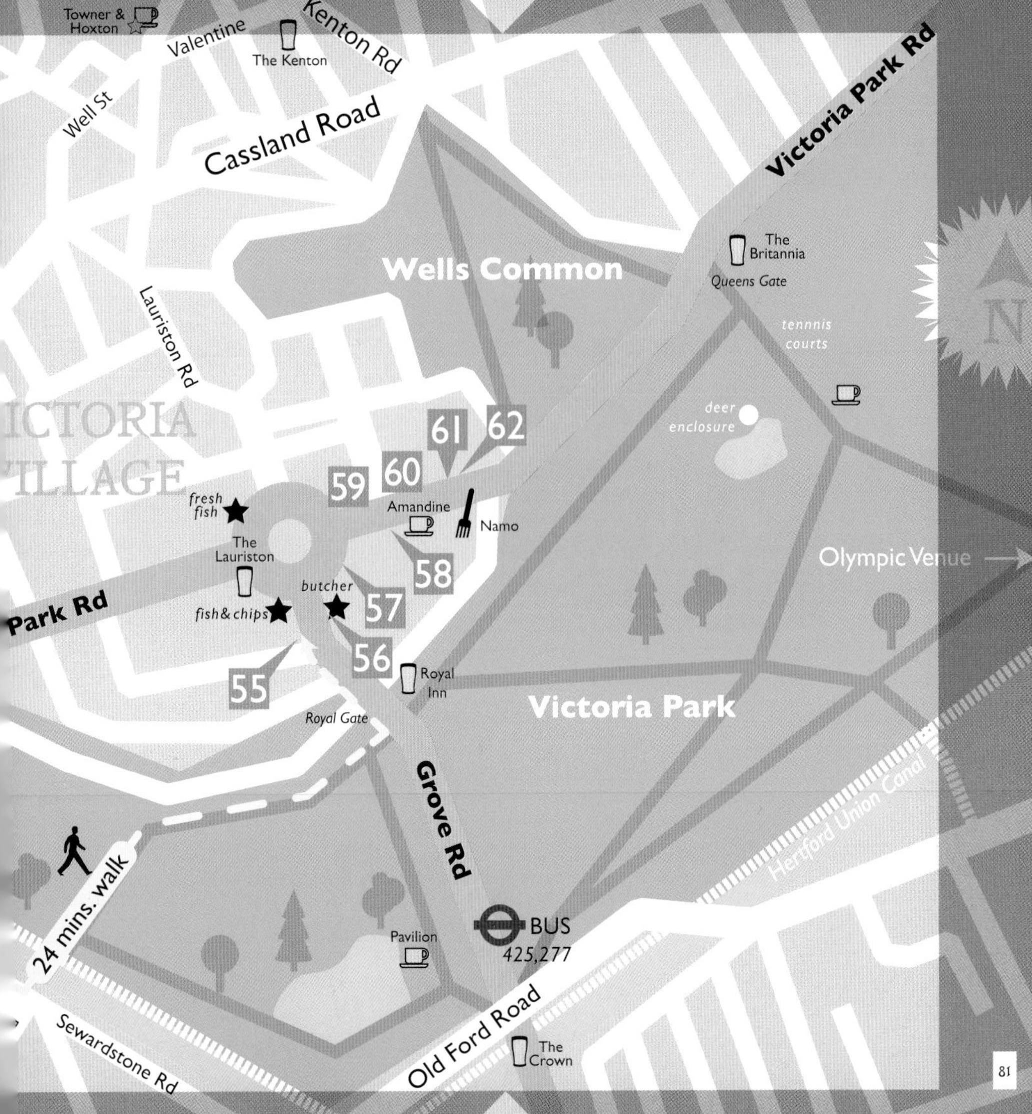

Towner & Hoxton
Valentine
The Kenton
Kenton Rd
Well St
Cassland Road
Victoria Park Rd
The Britannia
Queens Gate
Wells Common
tennnis courts
Lauriston Rd
ICTORIA
ILLAGE
deer enclosure
61
62
59
60
fresh fish
Amandine
Namo
The Lauriston
58
Olympic Venue
butcher
Park Rd
fish&chips
57
56
Royal Inn
55
Royal Gate
Victoria Park
Grove Rd
Hertford Union Canal
24 mins. walk
BUS
425,277
Pavilion
Old Ford Road
Sewardstone Rd
The Crown
N

Maison Bertaux Soho (Page 108)

WC1 Lamb's Conduit Street
WC2 Covent Garden
W1 Soho
W2 Connaught Village
W2 Portman Square
W1 Jermyn Street
SW1 Belgravia
SW1 Pimlico

Tania, curator of the **Maison Bertaux Gallery**, at the time of printing playing host to Noel Fielding (the mighty bouche), whose work was brilliantly displayed throughout the warren like café, with Noel himself coming in regularly to make additions to his work on the walls!

The People's Supermarket

In an area with such a diverse population encompassing those from council estates to millionaire homes, it's hard to cater for all. However in an efficacious way **The People's Supermarket** manages to achieve this. A co-operative enterprise where the locals pay a minimal membership fee to gain discounts on purchases and with a staff manned by volunteers it's a virtuous endeavour to maintain the consistency of Independent shops on the street. The store is designed to gratify those who want a loaf of sliced white to those that want rye sourdough with pumpkin seeds and where you will find Coca Cola sitting next to the finest organic apple juice. This lack of structure adds a huge amount of charm. A recent addition popular with locals is the in house kitchen taking fruit and vegetables on the turn to create delicious soups, stews and lasagne so nothing goes to waste. *PB*

MAP 6 Ref. 6

The People's Supermarket
72-78 Lamb's Conduit Street
WC1N 3LP
+44 (0)20 7430 1827
www.thepeoplessupermarket.org
Mon–Sat 8–9pm
Sun 10–6pm

If, like going to the dentist, hair salons make you nervous, then you will feel right at home at **Badlamb's & Sons**. Like walking into a Rockabilly's living room with shelves of art books, CDs, inanimate objects and the odd bottle of wine it's certainly a home away from home. Having been in the business for over 20 years, Tony has carved himself a nice little niche with his Italian barbershop-esque salon. Charmingly makeshift, the red painted floorboards, old-fashioned barber chairs, red velvet curtains and painted wall murals of 1940's jazz musicians certainly lend an air of nostalgia. With a romantic history in hairdressing, Tony has done his fair share of impromptu late night cuts for artists and the like on the scene including working with Speigletent, a 1920's Cabaret tent. An eclectic selection of paintings and illustrations from "A Little Bit Of Art Ltd." complete the creative look of the shop. *PB*

MAP 6 Ref. 1
Badlamb's & Sons
37 Lamb's Conduit Street
Bloomsbury WC1N 3NG
+44 (0)20 7242 7573
www.badlambs.com
Mon–Fri 11–7pm
except Thu 11–8pm
Sat 11–5pm

Ben Pentreath

There is something so familiar about **Ben Pentreath**, perhaps it's the nostalgic paintings of the English countryside by wartime artist Eric Ravillious or the curious sideboard dishes made from old stamps set in resin. An interior architect by trade, Ben set up shop selling beautiful and interesting things that inspired him. Working in close collaboration with Bridie who introduces her love of curiosities to the shop, they have created a den of English treasures, including a large selection of plaster mouldings cast from a personal collection of antiques. Victorian domes and glassware in bright sapphire and ruby colours interspersed with eclectic and elegant modern table lamps by Mariana Kennedy who combines bookcloth lampshades with almost fluorescent resin bases. Giant log baskets made from woven rattan flank the entrance where geological survey maps of England and Wales feature alongside traditional kitchenware, shovels, feather dusters and heavy glass tumblers and sherry glasses sit atop antique furniture. *PB*

MAP 6 Ref. 3

Ben Pentreath Ltd
17 Rugby Street
Bloomsbury WC1N 3QT
+44 (0)20 7430 2526
www.benpetreath.com
Mon–Sat 11–6pm

Darkroom

Some might say it's a pretty bold move painting a shop black and white, however, I doubt any would argue that it's certainly an effective way to showcase the sculptural wares they have on display. Essentially selling accessories, whether for fashion or the home, **Darkroom** explores materials and their uses, selling soft leather bags with a fine wood trim or wall hangings made of heavy wool appearing like oversized pieces of jewellery. With backgrounds in fashion and interiors a lot of time goes into curating the store with the theme changing seasonally and in conjunction with the designers they work with, many of whom draw inspiration from Africa in a modernist way. Monochrome paintings line the wall evoking illusions of black mirrors and solid black plinths off-set against a geometric patterned floor display covetable gold and silver jewellery, and tribal themed accessories mixed with woven leather belts and conspicuous homewares. *PB*

MAP 6 Ref. 2

Darkroom
52 Lamb's Conduit Street
Bloomsbury WC1N 3LL
+44 (0)20 7831 7244
www.darkroomlondon.com
Mon–Fri 11–7pm
Sat 11–6pm

*Discount**

Maggie Owen

It was on a trip to the south of France some while back that **Maggie Owen** came across a beautiful beaded necklace. It was with this necklace and its unusual sculptural quality that she was inspired to open her own shop in this unique former dairy. Although her main focus is on costume jewellery primarily from renowned Parisian designer Philippe Ferrandis, her love of sculpture and anything jewel-like is evident throughout the store. Unusual beaded animals from a womens' collective in Cape Town are mixed with ethnic and regal semi-precious necklaces, earrings and bracelets in ethereal colours and fantastical designs. A striking silk piece from textile designer Margot Selby adorns the wall and fanciful balsa wood sculptures of the Eiffel tower from a Chinese supermarket in Madrid are intermittently placed amongst Faber and Faber books with beautiful covers and stacks of fashion magazines. *PB*

MAP 6 Ref. 4

Maggie Owen
13 Rugby Street
Bloomsbury WC1N 3QT
+44 (0)20 7404 7070
www.maggieowenlondon.com
Mon–Sat 11–6pm

Margo Selby

Like walking into a kaleidoscope **Margo Selby** is a blast of striking colour and geometric pattern. Brightly coloured cashmere scarves and silk fabrics with designs so textured they look three-dimensional and colours so vivid they are virtually fluorescent. A well established weaver Margo describes herself as a craftswoman first and a business woman second believing that handwoven qualities are too special to let die out. All the products sold in the store, from bedspreads to purses, buttons and ties are made in the atelier in the basement where the handloom is constantly whirring. Margo treats rugs and textiles like paintings, adoringly putting colours together creating theatrical and luxurious designs with books of sensational fabric swatches where customers can take their pick from various silks and upholstery fabrics. And it doesn't stop there; fun gift cards, coasters, mugs and plates emblazoned with the famous London landmark Trellik Tower complete the collection. *PB*

MAP 6 Ref. 7
Margo Selby
4–11 Galen Place
Pied Bull Yard
Bloomsbury WC1A 2JR
+44 (0)20 7242 6322
www.margoselby.com
Mon–Sat 10–6pm

Something

From time to time we are all faced with the inevitable problem, "What present should I get? I have to get *something*...". An apt name as '**Something**' will certainly have a suitable present for every occasion. A truly girly gift shop you will find some kind of charming object for every room of the house. Whether it's cookery books, enamel tins for the kitchen, Venetian glass mirrors and pretty tealight holders for the living room, delicious scented candles for the bedroom, or retro gardening tools for the girl with a new hobby, you won't fail. Like a mini department store of gifts you will find everything from inspired greetings cards made from old vintage playing cards to world map printed wrapping paper. The choice appears endless, including soft leather purses, picture frames, body products, children's clothes and toys and eclectic jewellery, says owner Toni, "I just don't know when to stop buying things". *PB*

MAP 6 Ref. 5

Something
58 Lamb's Conduit Street
Bloomsbury WC1N 3LW
+44 (0)20 7430 1516
www.something-shop.com
Mon–Fri 10.30–6pm
Sat 11–5pm
Open on Sun in Dec

Kidrobot

Have you ever been to a Japanese toy shop? Well here's a taster. **Kidrobot** produces limited edition art toys which have developed a serious cult following. Adored by both adults and children alike as they are both highly collectable and colourful, these 'toys' all come in bright and delicious packaging, too good to take out of the box. Inspired by 'Gashapon' vending machines in Japan, the smaller items Kidrobot produces such as key chains, mini figures and zipper pulls are 'blind box' so you never know which one you are actually getting. The chance is written on the box so you know if you have a 10/50 chance or a 1/50 chance and this is where the fun lies. One of their signature themes is Munnyworld, a series of super smooth vinyl figures, each one a blank canvas which comes with an accessory and a marker pen ready to impose your imagination on. *PB*

MAP 7 Ref. 19
Kidrobot
19 Earlham Street
Seven Dials WC2H 9LL
+44 (0)20 7836 4074
www.kidrobot.com
Mon–Sat 10–8pm
Sun 12–6pm

Mint

Mint is a breed of vintage shop that can actually call itself a vintage shop rather than just second hand, they don't buy in bags of clothes by weight here, everything is hand selected and whether it's an early 1980's denim jacket or a late 1980's one matters a great deal. A well-edited collection, they sift through hundreds of pieces to get to the perfect fifty. By closely following catwalk and street trends, suppliers are contacted in order to claim everything they predict will come into fashion. Garments must be in near-perfect condition and original, meaning Hawaiian shirts must be made in Hawaii with no missing buttons, no stains and no tears, so you will be buying as good as new. Leather jackets, thick wool jumpers, Swiss army backpacks, blazers and ankle boots are in abundance as; "sometimes we do a mass of one thing to show a bit of commitment". *PB*

MAP 7 Ref. 17
Mint
20 Earlham Street
Seven Dials WC2H 9LN
+44 (0)20 7836 3440
www.mintvintage.co.uk
Mon–Wed 11–7pm
Thu¬–Sat 11–8pm
Sun 12–6pm

Orbital Comics

Comic book shops can be intimidating and probably not the first stop on the list for those who don't wear an anorak. However, **Orbital Comics** has a totally different ambience than most comic shops as it feels more like a hang-out than a corporate merchandising machine; somewhere even those with a mild interest can pick up tips even if it's just for a love of the artwork alone. As the biggest stockist of vintage comics, Orbital has all the big name classics from Marvel and DC to a great selection of Indie and Manga along with hard to find back-issues and graphic novels. Continuing their homely feel is the homemade comics rack where people can create and sell their own titles at low prices, a nice alternative to the mainstream books. With a large gallery space, Orbital regularly hosts signings and events giving an opportunity to pick up a piece of comic history. *PB*

MAP 7 Ref. 22
Orbital Comics
8 Great Newport Street
Covent Garden WC2H 7JA
+44 (0)20 7240 0591
www.orbitalcomics.com
Mon–Sat 10.30–7pm
Sun 11.30–5pm

Super Superficial

Super Superficial is about two things; a love of t-shirts and a love of artists. Shelves lined with immaculately folded sweatshirts, hoodies and t-shirts, emblazoned with exciting street art inspired illustrations, photographs and artworks from the likes of Chris Dent and Will Thompson, all just as worthy to be framed as worn, create a mutually beneficial environment for fashion and art to co-exist. This way artists get more exposure as each garment becomes a talking piece. A straightforward idea, each t-shirt design is by a different artist with new releases each month keeping the collection current and inspired. Downstairs they have a bright art space showcasing established artists next to emerging artists, "the idea being that they are mentioned in the same sentence" creating a great platform for graduates to showcase their work and gain recognition. *PB*

MAP 7 Ref. 18
Super Superficial
22 Earlham Street
Seven Dials WC2H 9LN
+44 (0)20 7287 7447
www.supersuperficial.com
Mon–Sat 11–7pm
Sun 12–5pm

Tatty Devine

If you were to have a root through the jewellery collection of any stylish London girl, chances are you will come across at least one piece by **Tatty Devine.** Creators of witty and fun Perspex pieces, Tatty Devine are well known in fashionable circles for their quirky necklaces, earrings and bracelets. Here you will find beautifully crafted jewellery such as mirrored angel wing and heart-shaped lollipop necklaces next to crown and bow shaped rings. Keen to be involved in other creative endeavours, Tatty Devine have done various commissioned projects creating unique and collectable pieces in collaboration with other artists such as gin bottle shaped pendants for a Gilbert and George travelling show and a Roller-skate pendant as they are the proud sponsors of the 'London Rollergirls'. The collection is complemented by a selection of girly 50's shoes and hats by the likes of Swedish brand Minimarket. *PB*

MAP 7 Ref. 21

Tatty Divine
44 Monmouth Street
Seven Dials WC2H 9EP
+44 (0)20 7836 2685
www.tattydivine.com
Mon–Sat 11–7pm
Sun 12–5pm
Late night Thu until 8pm

Unconditional

Where should you go if you're a busy person who needs to be comfortable and stylish from when you get dressed in the morning to cocktails at the end of the day? **Unconditional** that's where. Experts in creating rock chic pieces for both men and women using subtle colours and flattering drapery in super soft fabrics, they make dressing look effortless. With an unfussy androgynous aesthetic, which accommodates most body shapes, this is sophisticated dressing to a T. Although the shop features mainly their own label they also stock a witty range by JC de Castelbajac with bags, shoes, shirts and knitwear emblazoned with Bambi and characters from Southpark. Additionally they also have a great range of jewellery with giant glitzy diamante gems and pale pink skulls on fine silver chains. An offbeat store with various curiosities including taxidermy rabbit heads with antlers it's a fantastic shop for those who like to reside in distinguished comfort. *PB*

MAP 7 Ref. 20

Unconditional
16 Monmouth Street
Seven Dials WC2H 9DD
+44 (0)20 7836 6931
www.unconditional.uk.com
Mon–Sat 11–7pm
Sun 12–6pm
Late night Thu until 8pm

Aram Store

'Hospital furniture' is what the public called the modern furniture from Le Corbusier, Castiglioni and Le Breuer, Zeev Aram had put on display in his tiny King's Road showroom. That was circa 1964. Almost fifty years later, **Aram** is now considered a design guru, the one who introduced along with Terence Conran of Habitat the idea of decorating your house with something else other than chintz. Since then, he may have expanded to bigger premises, like this 5-storey converted warehouse in Covent Garden. But he hasn't lost any of his insatiable passion for modern design, and along with his children, Ruth and Daniel, has never ceased to stock some of the biggest names in design. There may be some hefty price tags involved, yet the best thing is that you can just wander around in the shop's beautifully curated showroom. You can't put a price on that, for sure! *DG*

MAP 7 Ref. 26
Aram Store
110 Drury Lane
Covent Garden WC2B 5SG
+44 (0)20 7557 7557
www.aram.co.uk
Mon–Sat 10–6pm
Late night Thu until 7pm

Laird London

It's great when someone fills a gap in the market isn't it! This can be said for **Laird**, suppliers of expertly made traditional hats of every different variety; from Baker boy, Flat-cap and Pork pie to Top Hat, Panama, Trilby and Sherlock Holmes. Established due to a love of hats and the lack of quality men's headwear, Laird realised the importance of opening a shop dedicated to the one fashion item which "completes an outfit, hats are a bold statement, they can completely change a look". Until Laird opened up, good quality hats were hard to come by, everything was either very dull or very expensive. With a good cross section of classic hats of exceptional quality, they do limited runs and on different occasions produce each type of hat in different fabrics for those with a penchant for a particular style. *PB*

MAP 7 Ref. 23
Laird
23 New Row
Covent Garden WC2N 4LA
+44 (0)20 7240 4240
www.lairdlondon.co.uk
Mon–Sat 11–7pm
Sun 12–6pm

McClintock Eyewear

Thanks to the latest 50s revival, geek glasses are back in fashion. But if you want to go one step beyond the current trend, Seamus **McClintock** is the guy for you. Having worked for over sixteen years in the eyewear industry (in design and retail respectively), McClintock has created a shrine to the 'bespectacled look' with his eponymous and original 'McClintock' boutique. Expect some amazing optical frames from unique designers: wooden styles by Made, colourful and modern frames by Kirk Originals or Kilsgaard, and even 50s-inspired styles by Patty Paillette. Whether you want a cool Buddy Holly look or even something inspired by Bauhaus architecture, here you will be spoilt for choice. Even though the shop stocks a huge variety of different styles, what they all have in common is the fact that they are unique, innovative and handmade. The same principle applies to sunglasses. For your eyes only. *DG*

MAP 7 Ref. 25
McClintock Eyewear
29 Floral Street
Covent Garden WC2E 9DP
+44 (0)20 7240 5055
www.mcclintock-eyewear.co.uk
Mon–Sat 11–7pm
Sun 12–5pm

Tenderproduct

You have to love the fact that there is a place in London to buy 'cut out pets', yes that is an actual thing. **Tenderproduct** hosts a carefully selected collection of quirky designs, Russian doll shaped USB sticks, key chains handmade out of worn down coloured pencils and Japanese hand-stitched soft toys using re-claimed fabric so no two are the same, accompanied by their own personal story. The product shop grew from the gallery two doors down which focuses on giving young artists their first solo show. Having featured several artists who worked in miniature, the idea came about to open a shop where designers could create affordable products and explore ideas. They feature a few mass produced items all of which however, credit the designer, keeping with their independent theme. Additionally they have a small gallery space downstairs tying in the pure artistic element. *PB*

MAP 7 Ref. 25

Tenderproduct
6 Cecil Court
Covent Garden WC2N 4HE
+44 (0)20 7379 9464
www.tenderproduct.com
Tue–Sat 10–6pm

*Discount**

Sir Tom Baker

Fashion . Soho

For sartorial elegance with an edge, tailor to rock stars **Sir Tom Baker** is your man. Handmade bespoke as well as off the peg there is a finally cut suit here for even the most requiring gentlemen. All based on that classic English cut.

MAP 7

Sir Tom Baker
4 D'Arblay Street
Soho W1
+44 (0)20 7437 3366
www.tombakerlondon.com
Mon–Fri 11–7pm
Sat 10–6pm

Fernandez & Wells

'We don't serve soya milk here, we're purists!' A statement which sums up what **Fernandez & Wells** is all about, although I can assure you it was said in good humour. This stylish, uncluttered and utilitarian café with rustic wood floorboards and aluminium stools is a popular Soho spot packed from open to close and for good reason. Sandwiches, coffee and cakes. If you're looking for something along the lines of 'rare topside of beef with horseradish and rocket' or 'roast pork belly with apple sauce' then you've come to the right place. Everything is fresh and well sourced. The coffee is excellent and lovingly prepared with the option of a selection of delicious Portuguese custard tarts and homemade almond and clementine loaf. And it doesn't stop there. Around the corner they have a food and wine bar where you can indulge in a variety of expertly picked wines, cured meats, cheese and bread. *PB*

MAP 7 Ref. 11
Fernandez & Wells
43 Lexington Street
Soho W1F 9AL
+44 (0)20 7287 8124
www.fernandezandwells.com
Mon–Sun 11–11pm

Frost French

With dusty pink walls covered in colour photocopies of fashion editorial spreads and boudoir style changing rooms with thick velvet drapes, it's a teenage girl's dream bedroom! **Frost French** is the creation of Londoners and life-long friends Sadie Frost and Jemima French who design fun and flirty yet sophisticated clothes for women who love to dress up. With a huge celebrity following they count the London 'it' crowd including Kate Moss, Lily Cole and Pixie Geldof as friends and muses. But it's not just for the rich and famous, in-house stylists can make everyone look and feel like a star. Definitely worth a visit if only to look at the fun pictures and Polaroids of the designers with their friends. Or to pick up a teaset. A recent collaboration with Lipton Infusions saw the creation of glass teacups cheekily printed with fruity lipstick stains. *PB*

MAP 7 Ref. 15
Frost French
22 Noel Street
Soho W1F 8GS
+44 (0)20 7494 1701
www.frostfrench.com

Lewis Leathers

For members of the Clash, the Ramones and the Sex Pistols there was only one leather jacket to be worn and that was one by **Lewis Leathers**. Established in 1892 the company made protective clothing for the increasingly popular pursuits of motoring, motorcycling and flying, going on to make outfits for the RAF during World War II. Nostalgic posters and music ornament the shop along with old leather jackets embellished with patches and badges, flying helmets and well-worn leather biker boots.

Specialising in the mid fifties to late seventies period, the shop features rails of jackets for both men and women in varying styles with names such as 'Lightening' and 'Easy Rider' and boots still manufactured from original 1967 patterns. After the war with the affluent youth movement wanting to look like Marlon Brando in the Wild One the Bronx Jacket was created being an instant hit, securing Lewis Leathers in the Rockers hall of fame. *PB*

MAP 7 Ref. 16
Lewis Leathers
3-5 Whitfield Street
Fitzrovia W1T 2SA
+44 (0)20 7636 4314
www.lewisleathers.com
Mon–Sat 11–6pm

Machine-A

Located in a former tailors shop, **Machine-A** was established as a shop and gallery to showcase the bright and the bold of London's creative movement. A space that stocks clothes by young designers who won't compromise and aren't afraid to not be commercial, here you will find beautiful pieces usually only seen on the pages of avant-guard fashion magazines. Huge window spaces flank the entrance with what can only be described as bizarre installations by the likes of Charlie Le Mindu whose hanging bloody heads are controversial to say the least. The stock ranges from downright weird to utterly wearable and cool as hell and aims to accommodate those who want to stand out from the crowd and those that don't. Each month Charlie Le Mindu does a pop-up salon and the basement downstairs is used to host events such as new collection previews, artist exhibitions and film screenings. *PB*

MAP 7 Ref. 14

Machine-A
60 Berwick Street
Soho W1F 8SU
+44 (0)20 7998 3385
www.machine-a.com
Mon–Sat 11–7pm

*Discount**

Maison Bertaux

Café . Soho

Michele has been leading lady at **Maison Bertaux**, the wonderful patisserie deep in Soho for 18 years. Serving up sweet tarts washed down with rich coffee or fine tea. The community of local loyal regulars are testament to how they have taken this iconic café to their hearts.

MAP 7

28 Greek Street
Soho W1D 5DQ
+44 (0)20 7437 6007
www.maisonbertaux.com
Mon–Fri 8.30–5.30pm
Sat 10–5pm
Sun 10.30–4pm

Pokit

We need to take a few steps back to a time when being properly dressed was the norm. For those who aren't prepared to take out a second mortgage, **Pokit** specialise in affordable, casual, tailor-made suits. Adhering to a very British aesthetic using a range of good quality tweeds, corduroy, wool flannel and cotton twill they follow time-honoured British tailoring techniques where service is the same for both men and women. With no need for an appointment, you can just walk in off the street and take your pick from a selection of tailored trousers in all manner of colours and styles hung elegantly from copper pipes. They have a number of sample size jackets for customers to try on and an in-house stylist to advise on the fit and style of your bespoke suit, ready in two to three weeks. To complete the look see their range of leather bags, shoes and accessories. *PB*

MAP 7 Ref. 13
Pokit
132 Wardour Street
Soho W1F 8ZW
+44 (0)20 7434 2875
www.pokit.co.uk
Mon–Fri 11–7pm
Sat 11–5pm

Scoop

So, what is the difference between ice cream and gelato? Well after you have glimpsed the fluffy mountains of creamy and vibrantly coloured dessert you will be happy to know that gelato has both a lower sugar content and a lower fat content than ice cream so much so in fact it's practically a health food! Calling its product 'natural luxury gelato' **Scoop** uses top quality ingredients excluding any artificial colourings, flavourings or preservatives. Each flavour tells you where the core ingredient originates: chocolate from Madagascar and peppermint from Pan Calieri, Piedmont. Could anything sound so delicious as 'Tiramisu with genuine Italian Mascarpone cheese, espresso made from single origin coffee beans, Acacia honey and Marsala wine from Sicily' or 'Caramello with farm fresh raw milk and pure white sugar caramel'? And it's not just gelato. They also have crepes and Belgian waffles, milkshakes the not-quite-so-minimal chocolate and coconut dipped waffle cones with sprinkles! *PB*

MAP 7 Ref. 12

Scoop
53 Brewer Street
Soho W1F 9UJ
+44 (0)20 7494 3082
www.scoopgelato.com
Mon–Fri 12–10.30pm
Sat–Sun 12–11pm

Beyond the Valley

A true hub of creativity and innovation, there are no rules at **Beyond the Valley**, just so long as it's not ordinary. Homewares are interspersed with clothes, accessories, gifts and non-sequential items, such as knitted toys and ceramic boxes in the shape of biscuits, basically anything that takes their fancy really. Playful and quirky designs are printed onto ceramic mugs, plates and notebooks and brightly coloured screen prints furnish the silver and gold papered walls. A unique space showcasing young designer talent, Beyond the Valley features the cream of the crop of London's fashion, product and jewellery designers. Alongside a selection of wearable items and printed t-shirts you will find beautifully crafted clothes that challenge functionality, shoes that look like sculptures and cabinets displaying jewellery that combines precious metals with leather, ribbon, Perspex, flocking, wood, feathers and rope. *PB*

MAP 7 Ref. 9
Beyond the Valley
2 Newburgh Street
Carnaby W1F 7RD
+44 (0)20 7437 7338
www.beyondthevalley.com
Mon–Sat 11–7pm
Sun 12.30–5pm

Joy Everley

In need of a special piece of jewellery and Tiffany isn't your cup of tea? Then try one of the longest established shops on the block, **Joy Everley**. This mother and daughter duo make elegant and timeless pieces in traditional and eccentric designs using precious metals and a variety of different stones. There are hundreds of wonderfully detailed and whimsical charms to choose from including top hats, roller-skates and cowboy boots with a variety of different bracelets and necklaces. Other key elements to the collection include a more traditional range of wedding and engagement rings for those that want something simple but beautifully made and their sparkling cocktail rings and earrings will glamorize any outfit, Hollywood style. An elegant and understated shop with panelled walls, oriental rugs and chandeliers; this really is a treasure trove of jewellery with a piece suitable for every taste and occasion. *PB*

MAP 7 Ref. 10

Joy Everley
7 Newburgh Street
Carnaby W1F 7RH
+44 (0)20 7287 2792
www.joyeverley.co.uk
Mon–Sat 10.30–6.30pm
Thu late night till 7

The Great Frog

If Joe Perry or Slash were to advise you on what guitar to buy you'd listen to them wouldn't you? Well the same can be said for Nicki Sixx and Lemmy when it comes to jewellery. If members of Motley Crue and Motorhead claim **The Great Frog** is the greatest Rock n Roll jewellery shop in London well you'd be a fool to argue. Purveyors of bespoke jewellery for the great and the good of the heavy metal scene since 1972 it was a father to son hand-over affair. Each piece is hand-finished in the basement below the shop by a team of trained artisans headed by Reino, who was trained by his father from the age of fifteen. Black antique cabinets display human skulls and Hannya masks, mixed with heavy, precious metal pieces including Rhino head rings, crucifixes and skulls hanging on bulky chains embedded with deep purple amethyst stones. *PB*

MAP 7 Ref. 8
The Great Frog
10 Ganton Street
Carnaby W1F 7QR
+44 (0)20 7439 9357
www.thegreatfroglondon.com
Mon–Sat 10.30–6.30pm
Sun 12–5pm

Clark & Reilly

With paint-splattered canvas stretched across the floor, old cabinets of curiosities and stacks of elegant fabric, not to mention shelves full of books and artistic magazines, **Clark & Reilly** is like, for one moment you've stepped back in time. Finding yourself in this theatrical setting amongst chipped furniture, worn old armchairs and a reclaimed Macdonalds restaurant sign, you might wonder what kind of shop you've walked into. Bridget Dwyer and David Grocott travel the world seeking out treasured artefacts and textiles, refurbishing them and working closely with a team of artisans to create unique and inspired pieces. Romantics at heart they fall in love with the object, where it came from and who used it rather than the specific 'look'. They love giving new life to things and reworking vintage items, whether it's a chandelier made out of Victorian jelly moulds or a hooped underskirt now a ceiling lampshade, the possibilities are endless. *PB*

MAP 8 Ref. 31
Clark & Reilly
8 Porchester Place
Connaught Village
W2 2BS
+44 (0)20 7262 3500
www.clarkandreilly.com
Tue–Sat 10–6pm

Cocomaya

Cocomaya – like a scene from the movie 'Chocolat', this exquisite artisan chocolate shop brimming with colourful plates of dainty and elegant chocolates dusted in edible gold powder in unconventional flavours such as Earl Grey and lavender, certainly has a sense of humour. The creation of three fashion veterans, you have to love the irony of stands piled high with buttery pastries and delicious cakes, not to mention the rows of perfect truffles in fluorescent coloured wrappers. The adjoining café offers a delicious lunch with soup and salads from kiwi and tomato to fig, yogurt and Parma ham where they make everything from A-Z on the premises. Housed in a listed building, the rustic shelves stacked with bars of chocolate in irresistible packaging, embellished with colourful flowers and birds flecked with gold, and antique metallic pink cabinets full of vintage tea sets and Toby jugs certainly makes this the Christian Lacroix of chocolate shops. *PB*

MAP 8 Ref. 30

Cocomaya
12 Connaught Street
Connaught Village
W2 2AF
+44 (0)20 7706 2770
www.cocomaya.co.uk
Mon–Fri 7–7pm
Sat 8–7pm
Sun 8–6pm

Eliská

So your home or office is in need of a new look but it's important that it works around that 18th Century painting you inherited from your grandmother. Interior designer **Eliská** is a master of mixing old with new. Here you will find a grand collection of leather and antique silverware including a beautiful backgammon set, a 1900's travelling condiment case and a gentleman's crocodile skin toiletry bag complete with beaten sterling silver essentials. Her shop is a 'window' to her business, integrating her extraordinary finds, a collection of curious everyday things; candle sticks, coffee pots, toast racks all antique solid silver with a range of elegant scented candles and essential oils. Her style is aimed at a masculine audience, very black and white with splendid cowhide and patent leather topped table cloths and bespoke furniture. Nothing is off the peg and everything can be made to accommodate different desires. *PB*

MAP 8 Ref. 33

Eliská
16a New Quebec Street
Portman Village
W1H 7RU
+44 (0)20 7723 5521
www.eliskadesign.com
Mon–Fri 11–6pm

Establishment

Was it Patti Smith who said "The artist's job is to infuse magic into their creations"? As a former knitwear designer for John Galliano, Gail knows a few things about forging magic out of fashion. **Establishment** is like a giant girly wardrobe where you can take your pick from classic, elegant and avant garde pieces from Boudicca and JC Castelbajac interspersed with everyday wear and "car to bar" heels which are so high, walking may be a problem. The eclectic range comes from the concept that "as a shop owner you can curate things your own way not what the market dictates, it's not like I want the biggest slice of the pie". Here you will find everyday clothes, which are designed to help sculpt the body, it's not just any old pair of jeans. Downstairs is a by appointment only luxury vintage salon hosting some of the biggest names from Dior to Chanel. *PB*

MAP 8 Ref. 32

Establishment
11 Porchester Place
Connaught Village
W2 2BU
+44 (0)20 7402 8892
www.establishmentlondon.com
Mon–Fri 10–6.30pm
Sat 10–6pm

Purveyors of luxury loungewear, **Me&Em** design clothes that feel comfy, yet look fit to be worn to a cocktail party. Was there ever a greater invention I ask you? Using a base fabric known as 'Modal' a material 50% more water-absorbent than cotton they produce heavy yet super soft garments that are ideal around the house but totally respectable to collect the kids from school. They have an extensive range of cashmere, linen and jersey and include a few tailored 100% wool jersey pieces, orchestrated towards workwear. They keep the colour range versatile and simple, sticking with earthy tones, moss green, beige, black, grey and so on. In addition to their own collection they buy in brands that complement the look including everyday t-shirts, Falke tights and pretty ballerina pumps. *PB*

MAP 8 Ref. 28
Me&Em
21 Connaught Street
Connaught Village
W2 2AY
08456 800975
www.meandem.com
Mon–Sat 10–6pm
Thu late night till 8pm

Susannah Hunter

You wouldn't see many more varieties of flowers if you went to a florist! **Susannah Hunter** specialises in bags and furnishings all embellished with her distinctive trademark hand-appliquéd Nappa leather peonies, roses, tulips and daffodils. Her highly covetable bags (with an impressive celebrity fan base) are designed as useful shoppers using super-soft leather lined with thick velvet. After studying fashion at Central Saint Martins, Susanna resolved that she was more interested in details than clothes and that the thing she liked about bags was that they exist in their own right, they don't have to fit someone or come in different sizes, they are timeless pieces. Deciding that she wanted to master one thing that she could make her own she combined the three things she loved best: flowers, colour and drawing, with all her designs being translated directly from her drawings in sumptuous jewel colours. *PB*

MAP 8 Ref. 29
Susannah Hunter
19 Connaught Street
Connaught Village
W2 2AY
+44 (0)20 7402 5874
www.susannahhunter.com
Mon–Fri 10–6pm
Sat 11–5pm

Viola

It was after traipsing the streets of Paris and New York seeking out dens of iniquity, that Sara realised that what London lacked was enough one-stop fashion boutiques for clothes, accessories and other gorgeous bits and pieces to clutter up a dressing table. So with that she set up **Viola**. Here they stock a broad range of 'wardrobe solutions', wearable clothes (that can be put in the wash) for girls who like to layer, and unique pieces such as leather leggings and mad hand-printed trainers. With a background in specialist boutiques Sara knows a thing or two about good service as well. Viola works with people who create unique and interesting things whether it's pop art signs and screen-printed t-shirts or just people with an unbridled enthusiasm for what they do. Glamorous pieces are effective accents to the shop, all to the soundtrack of crazy retro Italian music. *PB*

MAP 8 Ref. 27
Viola
25 Connaught Street
Connaught Village
W2 2AY
+44 (0)20 7262 2722
www.violalondon.com
Mon–Sat 10.30–6pm

Jermyn Street/Trumper

A street with a lot of history and shops to match. Long known as a destination for an English gentleman to get 'fitted out', **Jermyn Street** is a fantastic area to explore with it's many shirtmakers and shoe shops some dating back Centuries. **Geo F Trumper** is one of the slightly younger of these establishments opened in the late 1800s on 9 Curzon Street (photo), it still retains the original early 20th century cubicles and mirrors. A second shop was opened on 20 Jermyn Street in the 60s. Other notable shops worth visiting on Jermyn Street include: New & Lingwood, no.53 (gentlemen's attire); Turnbull & Asser, no. 71 (shirts); Church's, no.108 &110 (shoes); Paxton & Whitfield since 1757 no.93 (cheese), Rowley's Restaurant, no.113; as well as the arcades that run between Piccadilly and Jermyn Street. Princes Arcade and Piccadilly Arcade. Nearby is Shepherds Market which is worth checking out too. Hidden away in Ormond Yard is the second White Cube gallery, a modernist cube of a building as if dropped from the sky into this secluded square.

(No Map for this area)

Geo F Trumper
20 Jermyn Street
May Fair W1J 5HQ
+44 (0)20 7734 1370
www.trumper.co.uk
Mon–Fri 9–5.30pm
Sat 9–5pm

Jermyn Street/Briggs the Barbers

Fylaktis Philippou (Philip to his friends), has been cutting the hair of MPs and Lords in St. James' for over 50 years. First becoming a barber as a boy in Cyprus in 1937, the shop is named after his former employer, Mr **Briggs**, who opened in 1917. Behind Jermyn Street just a few doors from an art gallery where John Lennon met Yoko Ono. He still cuts hair surrounded by photographs of home and family. He has just extended his lease, long may he continue.

(No Map for this area)

Briggs
5 Ormond Yard
May Fair SW1Y 6JT
+44 (0)20 7930 2070
Mon–Fri 9–4.30pm
Sat 9–4pm

Allegra Hicks is one of those people who know about good design because all their life they have been immersed in it. To start with, she grew up in a glass house, which was designed by her Italian architect father and was fully decorated with Gio Ponti's furniture. Then she studied design in Milan and Fine Art in Brussels and soon after she started designing frescoes in London. Ultimately it was textile and fashion design that won her over, with the establishment of her eponymous label. She may have recently moved to chic Belgravia, but one thing remains constant: her truly individual, eclectic and bohemian luxe style that defines up until today her fashion and interiors brand. Here you can find beautiful kaftans, elegant tops and dresses, as well as furnishings, upholstery and even notebooks in a range of the designer's distinctive prints, like her trademark 'Drop'. *DG*

MAP 9 Ref. 37
Allegra Hicks
42 Elizabeth Street
Belgravia SW1W 9NX
+44 (0)20 7730 3275
www.allegrahicks.com
Mon–Fri 10–6pm
Sat 11–6pm

Erickson Beamon

Karen Erickson and Vicki Beamon's jewellery business owes its beginnings to a shortage. While styling a runway show for another designer, they could't find the right jewellery to match the outfits, so they decided to make it themselves on the spot. Since 1983, when their eponymous label was established, the US-born duo have literally conquered the market with their trademark 'chokers' and their 'never afraid to make a statement' attitude. Big, chunky stone necklaces, floral designs, pearls, art deco pieces, bold bangles and earrings; maximalism at its best. The brand has now grown to cult status and has just recently added First Lady Michelle Obama to its loyal fan base, while it also counts in its CV collaborations with leading fashion houses. **Erickson Beamon**'s London outpost is a shrine to the duo's unique approach to jewellery design and statement pieces. One thing is for sure; you won't be able to just choose one. *DG*

MAP 9 Ref. 38
Erickson Beamon
38 Elizabeth Street
Belgravia SW1W 9NZ
+44 (0)20 7259 0202
www.ericksonbeamon.com
Mon–Fri 10–6pm
Sat 11–5pm

Joanna Wood

Joanna Wood is a well known name on Pimlico Road, and area in which she set up the shop 15 years ago. An established interior designer, especially known for a sophisticated and modern British take on interiors, Wood here offers interior accessories, furniture and furnishings, all reflecting her timeless style. What is great though is the real spirit behind her namesake shop: home objects, lights, furnishings and upholstery are all sourced from small independent suppliers in England and artisans found abroad, a feature which makes every purchase truly special. An ideal stop if you are on the hunt for a gift, here you will be amazed by the vast selection of ideas on offer: wonderful candles, cosy blankets, silk slippers, floral boxes, horn pen pots, at prices to fit all budgets. You will definitely feel tempted to keep them all for yourself. *DG*

MAP 9 Ref. 34
Joanna Wood
48a Pimlico Road
Belgravia SW1W 8LP
+44 (0)20 7730 5064
www.joannawood.co.uk
Mon–Fri 10–6pm
Sat 10–4pm

Ever wondered what the story is behind some of the most iconic or well known perfumes out there? Ever tried to find that elusive bottle of Tabac Blond or Serge Lutens' Feminite Du Bois? Head to **Les Senteurs** in Belgravia. This small, family-run emporium is the best place for perfumes - old favourites or new independent ones. Whether you are a perfume aficionado or someone who wants something new and fresh but above all something different from the mainstream celebrity endorsed offerings, Les Senteurs is the answer. The shop's friendly and very knowledgeable staff will take you through an olfactory experience, to help you find 'the One'. Of course if you can't make up your mind there and then, don't worry: their sample service, where you can take up to 6 mini vials back home, will enable you to choose the right potion at your own pace. *DG*

MAP 9 Ref. 36

Les Senteurs
71 Elizabeth Street
Belgravia SW1W 9PJ
+44 (0)20 7730 2322
www.lessenteurs.com
Mon–Sat 10–6pm

Tomasz Starzewski

Not every one can boast the late Princess Diana as one of their clients but **Tomasz Starzewski**, on the other hand, can. Not just her, but many more; from Baroness Thatcher to the model and Earl Spencer's former wife Victoria Lockwood. Starzewski has dressed them all in his unique and utterly elegant creations. Expect here a thoroughly classic and low key design sensibility for ladies of a certain kind (cocktail dresses, every day separates, eveningwear); above all expect an emphasis on superior quality. After all his mantra is «Glamour, elegance, good design, luxury'. His eponymous boutique reflects this in every sense with its minimal deco r, attention to detail and above all its commitment to friendly service. Suspended mannequins exhibit Starzewski's creations giving them a museum quality, while carefully placed blouses and separates grace the shelves. Nothing is superfluous, which is a case in point for Starzewski's discreet and timeless elegance. *DG*

MAP 9 Ref. 35

Tomasz Starzewski
97 Pimlico Road
Belgravia SW1 8PH
+44 (0)20 7730 5559
www.starzewski.com
Mon–Fri 10–6pm
Sat (By appointment only)

Ottolenghi (Page 195)

Peace camp Parliament Square 2010

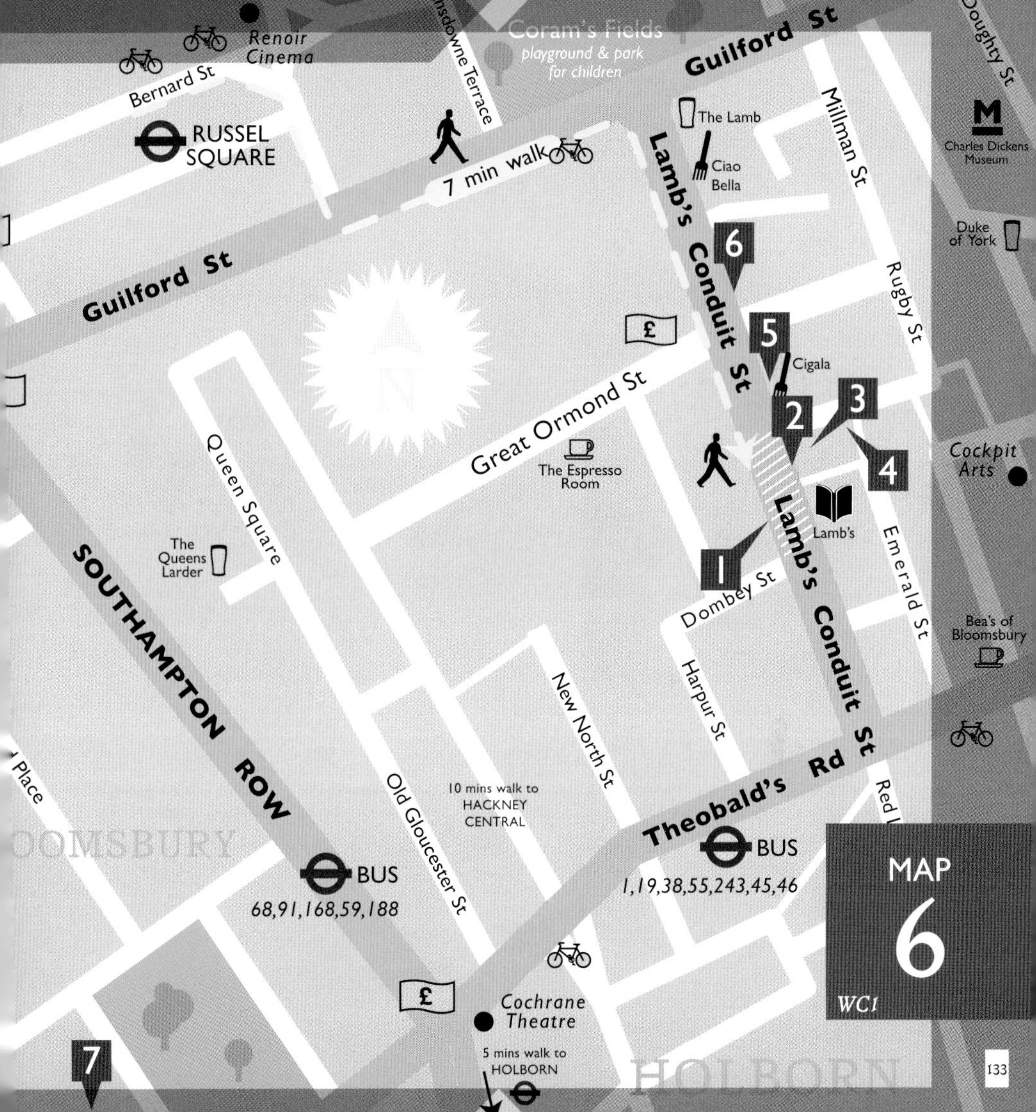
Renoir
Cinema
Coram's Fields
playground & park
for children
Guilford St
Doughty St
Bernard St
ansdowne Terrace
RUSSEL
SQUARE
The Lamb
Millman St
Charles Dickens
Museum
7 min walk
Lamb's Conduit St
Ciao
Bella
Duke
of York
6
Guilford St
Rugby St
5
Cigala
Great Ormond St
3
2
4
Cockpit
Arts
The Espresso
Room
Queen Square
Lamb's
The
Queens
Larder
1
Emerald St
SOUTHAMPTON ROW
Dombey St
Lamb's Conduit St
Bea's of
Bloomsbury
New North St
Harpur St
Place
Theobald's Rd
Red
10 mins walk to
HACKNEY
CENTRAL
Old Gloucester St
OOMSBURY
BUS
1,19,38,55,243,45,46
BUS
68,91,168,59,188
MAP
6
WC1
Cochrane
Theatre
5 mins walk to
HOLBORN
HOLBORN
7

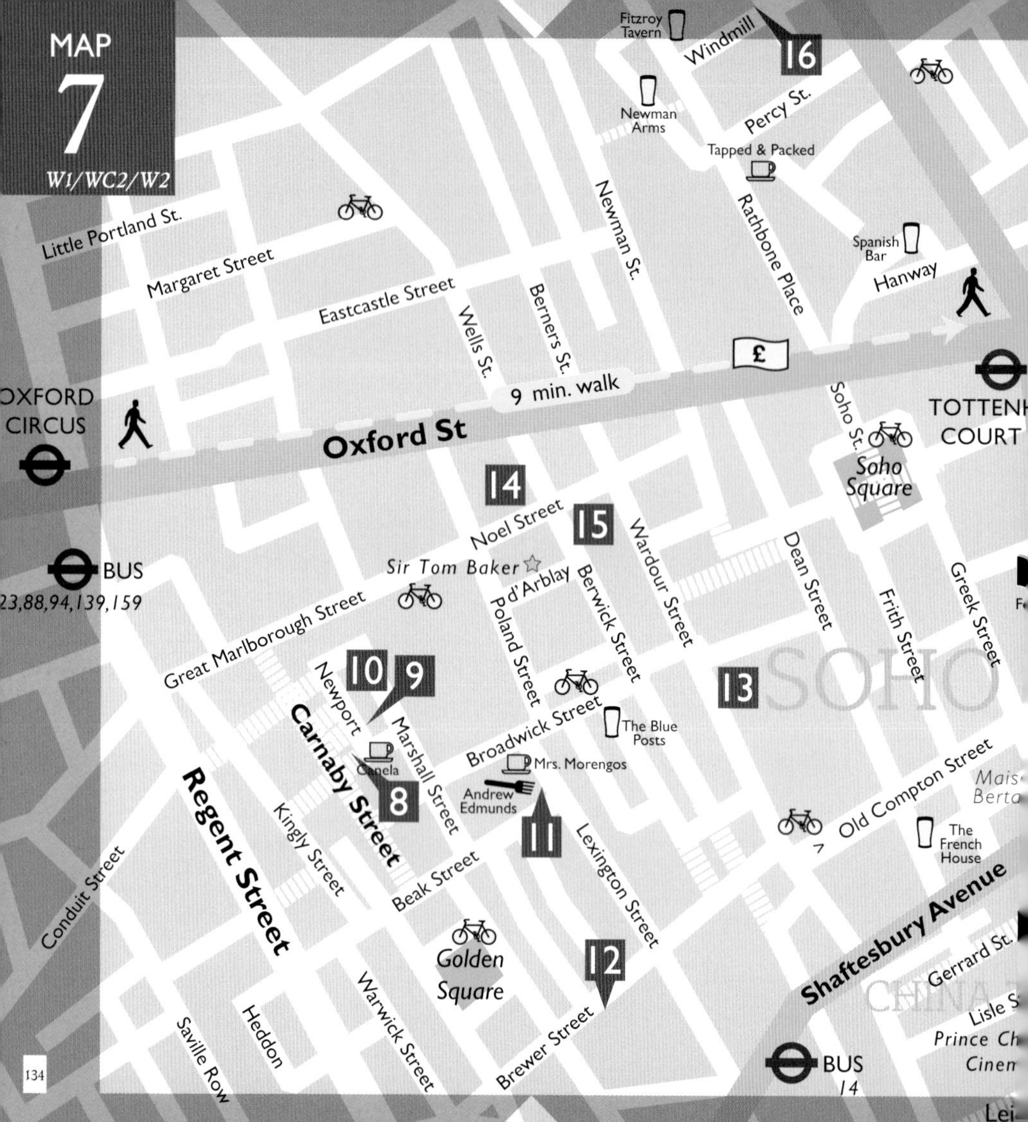

MAP
7
W1/WC2/W2
Fitzroy Tavern
Windmill
16
Newman Arms
Percy St.
Tapped & Packed
Little Portland St.
Margaret Street
Eastcastle Street
Wells St.
Berners St.
Newman St.
Rathbone Place
Spanish Bar
Hanway
9 min. walk
OXFORD CIRCUS
Oxford St
TOTTENH
COURT
Soho St.
Soho Square
14
15
Noel Street
Sir Tom Baker
d'Arblay
BUS
23,88,94,139,159
Great Marlborough Street
Poland Street
Berwick Street
Wardour Street
Dean Street
Frith Street
Greek Street
10
9
13
SOHO
Newport
Carnaby Street
Marshall Street
Broadwick Street
The Blue Posts
Canela
Mrs. Morengos
8
Andrew Edmunds
11
Old Compton Street
The French House
Regent Street
Kingly Street
Beak Street
Lexington Street
Conduit Street
Shaftesbury Avenue
Golden Square
12
Gerrard St.
CHINA
Lisle S
Prince Ch
Cinem
Warwick Street
Heddon
Saville Row
Brewer Street
BUS
14
Lei

Bloomsbury Street
British Museum
Museum Tavern
London Review
Camera Cafe
Cartoon Museum
Bi Won
Bloomsbury Way
BLOOMSBURY
BUS
New Oxford Street
Museum St.
BUS
1,8,19,55
HOLBORN
Kingsway
St. Giles High Street
Drury Lane
Rock & Sole
Endell Street
Monmouth
Shorts Gardens
Monmouth Street
20
19
Earlham St.
18
17
21
Shelton Street
Long Acre
COVENT GARDEN
Sarastro
Drury Lane
26
Opera House
Wellington St
Double Shot Coffee Co.
25
Floral Street
COVENT GARDEN
22
EICESTER SQUARE
King Street
Covent Garden Piazza
Henrietta St
Bou Tea
Tavistock St
BUS
8,9,13,15,23,91
Strand
23
24
St. Martins Lane
New Row
BUS
76
Cecil Ct.
Mas Burritos
CHARING CROSS

MAP 8

W2

BUS
16,N16,36,7,23,15

Sussex Ga
CONNAUGHT VILLAGE
Harrowby Street
George Street
Edgware Rd
Gt. Cumberland Pl
Seymour Pl.
Montagu St.
PORTMAN SQUARE
Cambridge Square
Oxford Square
Porchester Pl
Hyde Park Crescent
Radnor Pl
Kendal Street
31
30
32
Colbeh
Upper Berkeley Street
Grazing Goat
Imbiss
33
18 mins. walk
Duke of Kendal
Connaught St
Connaughts Cafe
Stanhope Terrace
Victoria
Streatham Pl
Hyde Park Street
Albion Street
Connaught Square
27
28
29
Seymour Street
Bryanston Stree
Clarendon Place
Brook Street
Hyde Park Gardens
MARB ARCH
Bayswater Rd
BUS
94,148,390
LANCASTER GATE
Cumberland Gate
Hyde Park

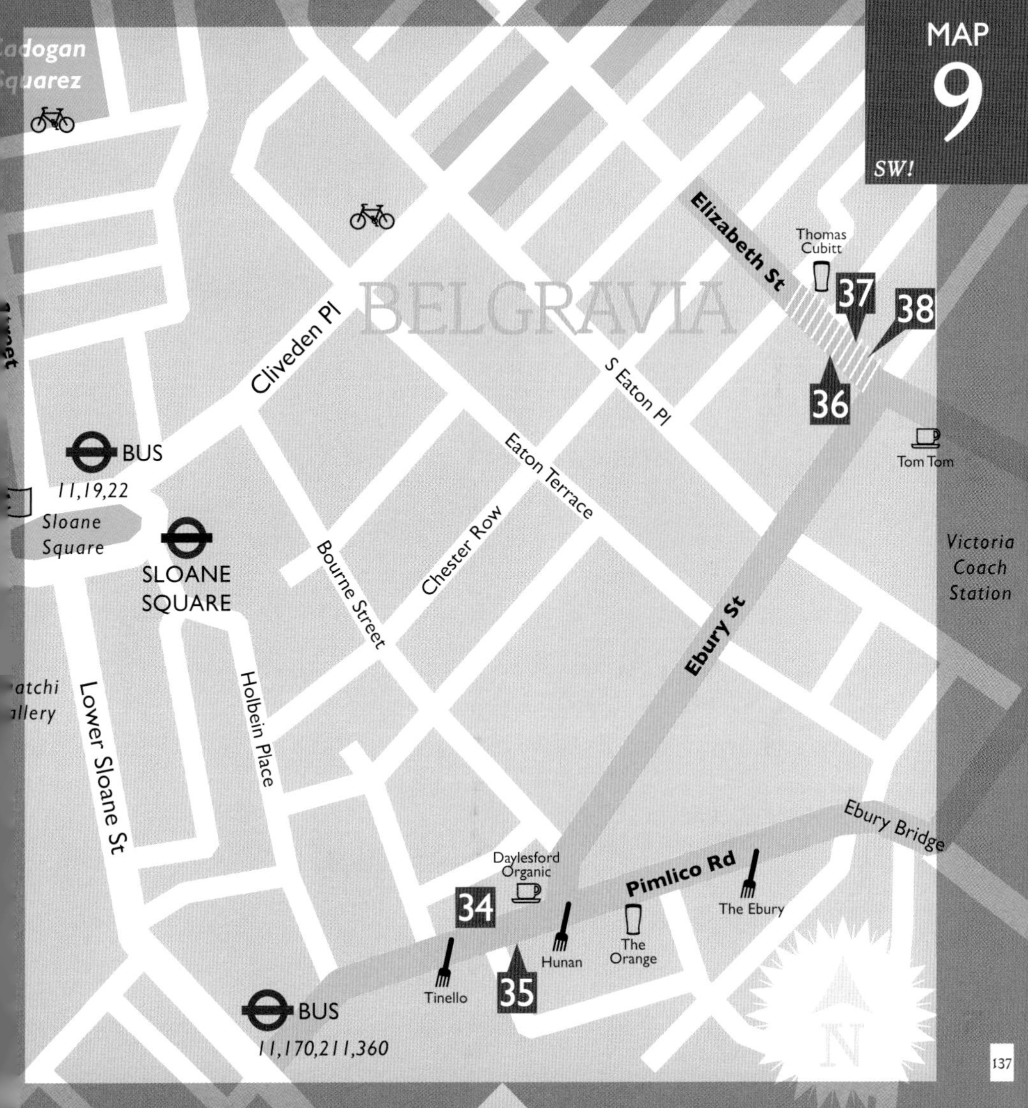
MAP
9
SW!
Cadogan Square
BELGRAVIA
Elizabeth St
Thomas Cubitt
37
38
36
S Eaton Pl
Tom Tom
Cliveden Pl
BUS
11,19,22
Sloane Square
SLOANE SQUARE
Eaton Terrace
Chester Row
Bourne Street
Victoria Coach Station
Ebury St
Holbein Place
Lower Sloane St
Ebury Bridge
Daylesford Organic
Pimlico Rd
The Ebury
34
Hunan
The Orange
Tinello
35
BUS
11,170,211,360
N

Circavintage www.circavintage.com

W11 **Notting Hill**
W8 **Kensington**
NW10 **Queens Park**
NW6/NW10 **Kensal Rise**
SW3 **Chelsea**
SW3 **Knightsbridge**
SW6 **Parsons Green**
SW6 **Fulham**

The rise of vintage, secondhand or retro however you want to describe them. It all seems to represent the same need for people seeking the original and one-off in an increasingly golbalised, mass production world. In West London visit **Circavintage** for all things Edwardian.

Ann Higgins

Anne Higgins describes her designs as 'medieval'. But don't let that fool you. What she means is wearable, vibrant, ethereal and earthy. Her knit designs have had a loyal following with writers, artists, scientists and healers for many years now due to their superior quality but also because she has also been a very well known figure in the area, having had shops on Portobello Road for over two decades. Higgins specialises in linen and wool garments, like dresses, ponchos and sweaters that are hand-knitted in workshops just outside London, using British yarns and rich silks, as well as elegant rubber macs for men and women. Her small outpost on Kensington Church Street is a testament to her creative spirit so it is no wonder her work has graced many exhibitions around Notting Hill as well as shows during the Edinburgh festival. *DG*

MAP 10 Ref. 3
Ann Higgins
107 Kensington Church Street
Notting Hill W11
+44 (0)7941 814221
Wed–Sat 11–5.30pm
and by appointment

Carter and Bond

Who would have thought that a four-year army stint would lay the foundation for a foray into the male grooming business? Joe Cotton was an Army Officer in the Cavalry, stationed in Germany and the Balkans for years. When faced with the everyday shaving regime and 'looking clean', as he puts it, he started looking for good quality skincare to counteract razorburn. "I was seeking out companies that could post products to various locations". 8 years on and his online emporium **Carter and Bond**, named after iconic male protagonists Jack Carter (Michael Caine in Get Carter) and James Bond, has expanded into a gentleman's shop which offers anything from barber services to various treatments along with a list of grooming products including Floris shaving soaps, Czech & Speake razors and Proraso after shave creams. "It is all about shaving" Cotton says. "Shaving is the holy grail for men." *DG*

MAP 11 Ref. 15
Carter and Bond
83 Westbourne Park Road
Notting Hill W2 5QH
+44 (0)20 7727 3141
www.carterandbond.com
Mon–Thu 9.30–6pm
Fri–Sat 9.30–7pm
Sun 11–5pm

-20%
*Off first wet shave**

Couverture & The Garbstore

On the outside, **Couveture & The Garbstore** may look like another cute 'Notting Hill' boutique, yet step in and you are quickly faced with a unique and thoroughly contemporary world of style that expands into three floors. Shopkeepers are Emily Dyson (daughter of James Dyson, of vacuum cleaner fame), and her husband Ian Paley (a former Paul Smith designer) and their ethos is all about offering a distinctive yet easy going view on fashion and style. A selected mix of international womenswear labels – A Detacher, Humanoid, to name a few – is on offer, as is Paley's own menswear brand, The Garbstore, together with accessories, children's and babywear, toys, jewellery and furniture. What is great about this concept store is its relaxed attitude; you are free to wander around and try its covetable and above all affordable finds in the safe knowledge that many of the sourced items are often only available in small quantities. *DG*

MAP 11 Ref. 11

Couverture & The Garbstore
188 Kensington Park Road
Notting Hill W11 2ES
+44 (0)20 7229 2178
www.couverture.co.uk
www.garbstore.co.uk
Mon–Sat 10am–6pm
Sun (Dec only) 12–5pm

Letizia di Guardo comes from a typical 'fashion' family: her grandfather worked as a tailor and her uncles own boutiques selling designers such as Versace and Gucci. But that didn't stop her from following a more a-typical fashion road: rather than selling the 'big guns' from her native Italy, she decided to open a boutique off Portobello Road, solely dedicated to 'independent' fashion. Featuring exclusive and lesser known names like Vivetta, Lorick, Tucker, Annalisa Cutore, Giuseppe Patane, all sourced from Italy, the United States and the UK, her ethos focuses on feminine, affordable womenswear and accessories with an emphasis on quality fabrics. After all, most pieces are handmade and unique using natural materials, like silk, georgette, crepe, cashmere, cotton and lace. Also **Di Guardo** is worth checking out for its cultural soirees and craft workshops, that include even knitting courses. *DG*

MAP 11 Ref. 12
Di Guardo
212 Kensington Park Road
Notting Hill W11 1NR
+44 (0)20 7243 9274
www.diguardo.co.uk
Mon–Sat 10–6pm
Sun 12–5pm

Gotham

Count on Dan Lonergan to bring his classic, sleek, pared-down spirit into UK homes and offices. **Gotham**, the interiors practice and lifestyle-shop which he opened more than a decade ago is now an institution for 1930s and '40s but also contemporary American-inspired furniture (think taupe colours and the classy appeal of ebony wood) for your home or office. He also offers a unique selection of home accessories, from bespoke carpets to chinoiseries, light fittings and even artwork for sophisticated city dwellers. Lonergan, a licenced architect himself, believes in simplifying the design process which is why his taste and services thoroughly abide by this straightforward attitude: 'Try it before you buy it'. *DG*

MAP 11 Ref. 9
Gotham
17 Chepstow Corner
1 Pembridge Villas
Notting Hill W2 4XE
+44 (0)20 7243 0011
www.gothamnottinghill.com
Mon–Fri 9–6pm
Sat 11–5pm

ilovegorgeous

Pretty but with an edge to it. That is how longtime best friends and savvy mums Lucy Enfield and Sophie Worthington describe their hippy chic childrenswear line, inspired by a trip to India, called **ilovegorgeous**. Having started out six years ago out of Enfield's Notting Hill kitchen, today their shop caters for discerning young bohemian princesses, ranging from 6 months to 15 year-olds. Their style is all about vintage-inspired beautiful dresses made of precious sari Indian fabrics, good quality cottons and viscose fabrics, pretty tops, dreamy coats and cashmere cardis with subtle retro details, but all devoid of loud colours and brash logos. The ever so popular Marie Antoinette-inspired smock dress (at £106) is guaranteed to make hardcore 'tomboys' change their mind. *DG*

MAP 11 Ref. 10

ilovegorgeous
52 Ledbury Road
Notting Hill W11 2AJ
+44 (0)20 7229 5855
www.ilovegorgeous.co.uk
Mon–Sat 10–6pm
Sun 12–6pm

'I was a divorce lawyer and friends joked I had gone from "home-wrecker to home-maker', says Elaine Williams of her leap from the dark corridors of the court to the stylish world of interior design, in which she has been working for the past 6 years. **Interior Couture** is her design studio-cum-impromptu 'gallery' space, in which she and her design team have carefully curated a collection of pieces of furniture, from 1940's Perspex and bronze chandeliers to beautifully handcrafted sofas and chairs, vintage fabric cushions, one-off pieces from new designers from the Royal College of Art, even some objets d'art and vintage furniture, gathered from their travels and trips to antique markets. The mix is as eclectic as ever but there is a reason. As Williams says, 'my ethos is all about being practical, comfortable, pleasing; interior design shouldn't be about a finished product on your door but should grow with the client.' *DG*

MAP 11 Ref. 14

Interior Couture
118 Talbot Road London
Notting Hill W11 1JR
+44 (0)20 7792 9775
www.interiorcouture.com
Mon–Fri 10–6pm
Sat 11–5pm
Sun 12–5pm

You have lived a bohemian life in Ibiza for ten years; your mother was a famous socialite and model turned human rights activist; Andy Warhol used to baby sit for you; your father is the lead singer of the Rolling Stones. If only **Jade Jagger** had been a writer... Yet, even in jewellery and fashion design, Jagger's rock 'n' roll heritage and haute hippy lifestyle seem to have found a good niche, that is why her first standalone shop, all dusky pink walls, dramatic black skirting and luxurious golden pillars and mirrors, is a shrine to that decadent, yet sumptuous and elegant spirit, which includes all a girl could ask for: a fine jewellery line (cue here, gold totemic skulls and safety pins) all made in India and with prices starting at £100), as well as a collection of beautiful beaded boho-luxe dresses. *DG*

MAP 11 Ref. 17
Jade Jagger
43 All Saints Road
Notting Hill W11 4HE
+44 (0)20 7221 3991
www.jadejagger.co.uk.
www.iwantjejebel.co.uk
Tue–Sat 12–7pm

Kokon To Zai

It may mean 'East meets West' in Japanese, but there is nothing Zen or civilised about **Kokon to Zai**. On the contrary, this fashion boutique is bordering on the bold, the surreal and the plain outrageous. You have never seen anything like this before. The 'child' of Marjan Pejoski and Sasha Bezovski, two Macedonian émigrés who came to study fashion design in London, Kokon to Zai opened its doors in 1996, originally as a space where DJs could hang out. Having gained cult status since then, Kokon to Zai now offers not just the designers' own labels 'Marjan Pejoski' (remember Bjork's famous swan dress?) and the flamboyant 'KTZ' but also a mix of clothes from fashion's most known provocateurs; Alexander McQueen, Vivienne Westwood and Jeremy Scott, to name but a few. All exhibited against a background of stuffed animals and antique paraphernalia making Kokon to Zai's eccentric microcosm an unforgettable experience. *DG*

MAP 11 Ref. 19

Kokon To Zai
86 Golborne Road
Notting Hill W10 5PS
+44 (0)20 8960 3736
www.kokontozai.co.uk
Mon–Sat 10–6pm

Lungta DeFancy

'A conceptual state of joy and happiness.' No, we are not talking about a new age religion, but rather about clothes. Well, you should never underestimate the joy they give. As its Tibetan-inspired name suggests, **Lungta de Fancy** is a journey through a glorious celebration of femininity, tailoring, and thus happiness, in the form of floaty chiffon dresses decorated with laser-cut appliqué designs, lurex kimonos, cute shift dresses and asymmetric coats whose collars can be also worn as belts.

'A cross between Vivienne Westwood's eccentricity and Comme des Garcons avant-garde spirit' is how the brand's designer, Mai Morimoto, describes the brand but don't expect anything wacky. This half-Japanese, half-Brit Morimoto has a great eye for creating ultra-sophisticated patterns that besides edgy, they are also wearable – but never 'mass produced'. As she says, every style is unique and comes only in maximum 20 pieces every season. With prices starting from £150, we suspect you will join this cult a.s.a.p. *DG*

MAP 11 Ref. 8
Lungta de Fancy
201 Westbourne Grove
Notting Hill W11 2SB
+44 (0)20 3417 6564
www.lungtadefancy.com
Mon–Fri 10.30–6.30
Sat 10–6.30
Sun 12–6

May

'I never liked zips, for some reason, or buttons.' says Peter **May**. That is why his womenswear collection features straightforward panels of fabric, which can be draped or tied around the body. 'It's easier that way,' he says. 'Not only you can be more imaginative but it's how you make a dress become truly yours.' May, who is a self-taught fashion designer, set up shop off Portobello after having worked for many prestigious fashion labels for years. His style is all about versatility and simple lines as well as a subversive attitude towards fashion: one size fits all. Here you can find an array of jersey, cotton, wool and silk dresses and tops, in a wearable palette of colours, like black, dark green, grey, navy blue and purple, all made using British fabrics as well as a range of leather accessories. Prices range from £95 to £285. *DG*

MAP 11 Ref. 18

May
61b Lancaster Road
Notting Hill W11 1QG
+44 (0)20 7229 2580
www.mayshop.co.uk
Mon–Sat 11–6pm
Sun 12–5pm

Oliver Goldsmith

Oliver Goldsmith has been described by the V&A Museum as the 'originator of fashion eyewear'. His designs have been worn by Hollywood's crème de la crème; Audrey Hepburn on Breakfast at Tiffany's, Michael Caine and Grace Kelly. Not only a shop, but more a haven for any eyewear enthusiast, Oliver Goldsmith has an extensive vintage archive of over 400 frames on display that customers can use as a reference for their own bespoke designs. Filled with nostalgic images of collaborations with the heroes of old Hollywood, it also serves as a history lesson on past fashions. Besides a bespoke service, with all frames being handmade in England and embossed with your name, if you want something extra, here you can also find the main collection of Oliver Goldsmith sunglasses, all replicas of their vintage designs as well as Claire Goldsmith's (Oliver's great grand-daughter) debut collection, called Legacy. *DG*

MAP 11 Ref. 16
Oliver Goldsmith
14 All Saints Road
Notting Hill W11 1HA
+44 (0)20 7460 0844
www.olivergoldsmith.com
Tue–Sat 10.30–6pm

Pedlars

Caroline and Charlie Gladstone (a great-great-grandson of the Prime Minister) may have quit the hustle and bustle of London 10 years ago and moved north to Glen Dye in Scotland, **Pedlars** HQ that is, but they chose W11 for their first lifestyle shop which opened in 2008. The husband and wife duo, capitalising on their background (Charlie, a former band manager for the Charlatans knows about funky things while Caroline, a former Laura Ashley designer, has a keen eye for colour) have been scouting the world for objects. Be it kitchenware, clothes or furniture that are functional but also quirky, industrial but witty, above all, objects that have 'heritage' and 'soul'; ergo British-made duffel coats, picnic baskets and Dualit toasters, even camping gear, handy for those summer music festivals. The shop has a mission statement which sums up the ethos: 'Stuff we love that you'll love too'. We couldn't agree more. *DG*

MAP 11 Ref. 13

Pedlars
128 Talbot Road
Notting Hill W11 1JA
+44 (0)20 7727 7799
www.pedlars.co.uk
Mon–Sat 10–6pm
Sun 11–5pm

Purple Bone

Enter **Purple Bone** and you'd think you have stepped into the wacky world of celebrity Hollywood pets or a 'Legally Blonde' scene. Do you remember Bruiser, Reese Witherspoon's adorable and super stylish yet spoiled chihuahua? Yet Purplebone caters not just to barking 'primadonnas' like Bruiser (a look at the treatments offered – Pawdicure or Dogzilian – will keep them satisfied for sure) but any pup worth its paws. Cue here, chemical-free shampoos and conditioners with coconut and papaya for their healthy and shiny coats, toys for stress-free afternoons and ergonomically designed food bowls for nice dinners. There is even a Purplebone club that will offer your special pup discounts with a card scheme so that he or she can earn redeemable points. Because they are worth it. *DG*

MAP 10 Ref. 4
Purple Bone
95 Notting Hill Gate
Notting Hill W11 3JZ
+44 (0)20 7985 0903
www.purplebone.com
Mon–Fri 9.30–7.00pm
Sat 9.30–6pm
Sun 12–5pm

Summerill & Bishop

If you ever wondered how you can give your kitchen that 'wow' factor or how you can organise the perfect dinner party, just head to **Summerill & Bishop**. Established in 1994 by longtime friends, June Summerill and Bernadette Bishop, this beautiful kitchen shop offers an amazing range of hand-crafted ceramics, bakeware, glassware, candles, monogrammed vintage linens and plates as well as some great utensils for the truly desering kitchen (think here, tarte tatin moulds and meat lifting forks).

Reflecting the allure and rustic elegance of the Provencal house or the laid-back charm of the Tuscany-style kitchen, most of the products are sourced accordingly; from France and Italy. The shop's highlight must be Its collection of 'art de la table' objects, which often include vintage finds from flea markets around Europe. As the owners say, 'it's often the little things in life that make the biggest difference.' We couldn't agree more. *DG*

MAP 10 Ref. 5
Summerill & Bishop
100 Portland Road
Holland Park W11 4LQ
+44 (0) 20 7221 4566
www.summerillandbishop.com
Mon–Sat 10–6pm

The Merchant

Sleek interiors, minimal decor, comfortable sofas: you'd think this was just another posh boutique for Notting Hill's boho elite. But don't let that fool you. **The Merchant** is actually a second-hand shop with a great selection of designer finds: Chanel, Gucci, Prada, Louis Vuitton but also Helmut Lang and Manolo Blahnik. Everything has passed the shop's quality control test, so do expect a lot of well kept pieces. There is even a waiting list for Hermes' Birkin bags. Capitalising on her experience as a globe-trotting personal shopper, Hamburg-born owner Vanessa Bunsen has a list of contacts who constantly feed her emporium with great stock. But with a twist: sellers have the option of donating part or all of their earnings to a preferred charity. Says Bunsen 'This way you know that when you buy anything from The Merchant, it will also benefit someone else'. A classic case of 'looking good by doing good'. *DG*

MAP 11 Ref. 6
The Merchant
36a Ledbury Road
Notting Hill W11 2AB
+44 (0)20 7229 1057
www.themerchant24.com
Mon–Sat 10.30–6pm
Sun 12–6pm

Wolf & Badger

Fashion's new-age Pygmalions Samir Ceric and Zoe Knight, are behind this new concept store, which is slowly becoming a Notting Hill establishment; in less than a year it has even won Vogue's prestigious 'Best Boutique' accolade. Its philosophy? Rather than exhibiting and selling established artists and designers, Ceric, an art gallery owner and his wife, Zoe, a successful accessories designer herself, have created a platform for fostering new talent freeing them from the financial worries of opening their own store, helping them even with distribution, manufacturing and press. Expect here a truly unique and idiosyncratic selection of womenswear, menswear to childrenswear and even home objects. *DG*

MAP 11 Ref. 7
Wolf & Badger
46 Ledbury Road
Notting Hill W11 2AB
+44 (0)20 7229 5698
www.wolfandbadger.com
Mon–Sat 10-6pm
Sun 11-5pm

Jimmie Martin

You want a beautifully carved baroque bed covered in silver leaf? Or a Louis XIV cabinet with a sprayed 'Imperfect' on it? Maybe a carver chair in Union Jack- inspired upholstery? Whatever your demand, turn to Jimmie Karlsson and Martin Nihlmar, of **Jimmie Martin**, for some luxury DIY. Their speciality is taking French style furniture and giving them the 'upcycle' spin, slightly quirky, slightly kitsch but thoroughly unique, which means they create one-off pieces which they customise with fun and funky new upholstery, finishes, hand-painted images and spray-painted graffiti. You can choose from an array of existing designs or request your own frame finish, upholstery and artwork. *DG*

MAP 10 Ref. 2
Jimmie Martin
77 Kensington Church Street
Kensington W8 4BG
+44 (0)20 7938 1852
www.jimmiemartin.co.uk
Mon–Fri 11–6pm
Sat 12–4pm

Pomegranate

'The main aesthetic at **Pomegranate** is clean simple lines and an emphasis on hand-crafted organic forms,' says Katie Bulatovic, owner of this gem of a jewellery shop, which she opened back in 2008. Beautiful silver bracelets, necklaces and rings with natural gemstones, like aquamarines and smokey quartz are a highlight. So is the price. Starting at just £15, people here can experiment with pieces that are different or pieces that work with current trends, without having to make a big investment – 'but still purchasing something in precious metal and set with gemstones; something that has an intrinsic value and a story behind it,' as Bulatovic puts it. Everything is sourced in India, Thailand and Turkey from local craftsmen and artisans, so expect a unique range of wonderful stones, techniques and styles. *DG*

MAP 10 Ref. 1

Pomegranate
8 Kensington Square
Kensington W8 5EP
+44 (0)20 7937 9735
www.pomegranate-london.co.uk
Mon–Sat 10–6pm
Sun 12–5pm

Eulabee is Verandah's younger sister. Opened in 2008, just around the corner from its predecessor, this magnificent emporium is based on the same principles: beautiful, retro and slightly quirky but above all affordable. Simone Russell and Penny Meachin have done a wonderful job at creating not just a shop but rather a funky and laid back lifestyle. The shop is superbly staged with all the objects on sale, which adds to Eulabee's thoroughly charming and slightly eccentric spirit. The focus here is on homeware (cushions, cake stands and other decorative objects as well as design books and even table games), while the whole experience feels like a fun day out: from the fake grass patch on the outside to the adjacent cafe where you can have a delicious lunch or enjoy a quick cup of coffee. Bonus: the shop is very child-friendly. *DG*

MAP 12 Ref. 24
Eulabee
116 College Road
Kensal Rise NW10 5HD
+44 (0)20 8968 5536
Mon–Sat 10–6pm
Sun 10–4pm

Kidsen

Corina Papadopoulou was an MTV producer before she opened one of London's most lovable children's boutiques. And she couldn't have found a better place to do it: after all, NW10 is a notorious Nappy Valley. Yet there is something different in her approach. "When I conceived the idea for **Kidsen**, I was heavily pregnant with my first child. Getting ready for my daughter's arrival, I was tired of shops which treat kids like grown-ups or ones that try to sell you everything" says this half-Greek, half-Swedish mother of two. That is why Kidsen, which opened in 2008, is not just a shop but more of 'a friendly community'. 'Here you can meet other mums and get advice on breastfeeding or the best nappies.' On top of that, Kidsen also stocks an eclectic range of Scandinavian baby- and childrenswear ('functional and practical without being ugly') as well as some wonderful toys. *DG*

MAP 12 Ref. 23
Kidsen
111 Chamberlayne Road
Kensal Rise NW10 3NS
+44 (0)20 8969 7565
www.kidsen.co.uk
Mon–Fri 10–5.30pm
Sat 10–5pm

Fashion designer Nelli Turner has already had a varied and interesting life; from an idyllic childhood in Bavaria to her studies at the Ecole Superieure d'Arts Appliques in Geneva and finally to her arrival in London, where she has worked for designer duo Clements Ribeiro. As such, her Kensal Rise boutique, **Lali**, is a testament to this unique lifestyle. Besides stocking her own Bi La Li womenswear brand, which she founded in 2001 (modern design and clean silhouettes are a signature style) Lali plays host to an amazing selection of young, savvy and original clothes, like Ghulam Sakina dresses, Eley Kishimoto and Osman Yousefzada separates, quirky jewellery by Tatty Devine and Mawi as well as Ally Cappelino accessories. Besides its unique retail offerings, here you can also find an array of objects from upcoming designers, design graduates and artists. In other words, a 'must see'. *DG*

MAP 12 Ref. 21

Lali
15 Station Terrace
Kensal Rise NW10
+44 (0)20 8968 9130
www.bilali.com
Tue–Thu 11–7pm
Fri–Sat 10–7pm
Sun 11–5pm

Retrouvius

Adam Hills and Maria Speake met as architecture students, got married and founded **Retrouvius**, an interior design practice and showroom with an interesting design manifesto: there is no such thing as waste. Case in point, their studio, which is made from reused materials and salvage. Hills, Speake and their team scour the UK for old buildings, be it soon-to-be demolished schools, galleries and even museums and take back anything that can be put into a new context; like the fossilised marble floor found at a demolished Heathrow terminal (which was subsequently made into a bathtub and a coffee table). Other reclaimed objects include cupboards, lighting, mirrors, as well as garden accessories. The great thing is that stock is ever changing, so chances are that you will find something unique and quirky, like the Central Line's old tube signs. Incredible to think that these were unwanted. *DG*

MAP 12 Ref. 20
Retrouvious
2A Ravensworth Road
Kensal Green NW10 5NR
+44 (0)20 8960 6060
www.retrouvious.com
Mon–Sat 10–6pm

Verandah

Friends Simone Russell and Penny Meachin have always wanted to create a shop with 'unusual but beautiful things'. So, having had a background in textiles and fashion design respectively, they opened **Verandah** back in 2000, a gorgeous little place full of beautiful gifts and treats as well as funky womenswear. Originally in Notting Hill, Verandah has since then moved to NW10 but has still retained its retro charm, quirky attitude and affordability factor. Here you will love the great selection of 'pocket money' ideas, such as lip salves, mirrored compacts, all starting at 50p, but also the amazing second-hand designer bargains.
The shop itself is an explosion of colour and patterns: the diamond-shaped print on the floor as well as the colourful treats Russell and Meachin have chosen for Verandah are simply a feast for the eyes. It helps that the latter are affordable, too. *DG*

MAP 12 Ref. 22

Verandah
117 Chamberlayne Road
Kensal Rise NW10 3NS
+44 (0)20 8968 5498
Mon–Sat 10–6pm
Sun 12–5pm

Aelia Laelia

Aelia Laelia is one of those retail institutions that have remained true to the original Chelsea spirit: a real independent boutique with unique designers who make fashion that extends beyond the current trends. This little treasure cave specialises in womenswear that is 'fun, happy, colourful and practical', as owner, Cathy Rayner, says. With a background in textile design and fashion sales, Rayner's ethos is all about offering quality brands that 'you can't find anywhere else', something which translates into timeless fashion from an eclectic and not widely available range of English, French and Danish names. Its speciality? Its extensive selection of great tops and dresses, with prices starting at just £49. Aelia Laelia is also known for its amazing holidaywear all year around; Star Mela kaftans, leather boho sandals, cute studded belts. Judging by its cool and laidback vibe, now we know why. *DG*

MAP 13 Ref. 29
Aelia Laelia
4 Cale Street
Chelsea SW3 3QU
+44 (0)20 7584 4400
Mon–Sat 10–6pm

A girl's heaven on earth! **Austique** is filled with utterly feminine clothes, fabulous jewellery, cheeky accessories and every day necessities: from Libelula dresses, Wilbur and Gussie's chic pochettes and Alex Monroe's bubblebee necklaces, to Seda France's scented candles, cashmere gloves, Essie nail varnishes and New York's infamous Dylan's Candy Bar goodies. The best thing? Its relaxed yet thoroughly glam atmosphere. It feels like you are in your private boudoir, sharing secrets and tips with your best friend just before a great night out. Owners are sisters Lindy Lopes and Katie Canvin, who opened Austique back in 2004 and whose aim was to introduce niche Australian brands into the habits of style conscious Chelsea girls. Since then, Austique has grown into a prime destination for original and thoroughly feminine fashion brands. *DG*

MAP 13 Ref. 32
Austique
330 King's Road
Chelsea SW3 5UR
+44 (0)20 7376 4555
www.austique.co.uk
Mon–Sat 10:30–7pm
Sun 12–5pm

Felt

If you are looking for something special – that eternity ring with those ethically sourced uncut gemstones by Pippa Small, or that one of a kind necklace with oversized links by Taher Chemirik, even those vintage 18-carat gold earrings - but you don't have the time to visit hidden away shops and faraway studios or the strength to do the flea market scene, just head over to **Felt**, an Alladin's cave but for jewellery. Its owner Eliza Poklewski Koziell, a specialist who used to work for auction/vintage obsessed entrepreneurs, has selected designers who may be lesser known but they nevertheless feature a unique design sensibility. What is great about Felt is also the fact that it is unassuming and casual; jewellery is treated not as something to be marvelled at from afar or behind glass cases but rather something that you should try on and make work for you. Prices range from £20 to £10,000, while you can also sell your old jewellery through the shop and get a credit for the amount they were sold for. *DG*

MAP 13 Ref. 30
Felt
13 Cale Street
Chelsea SW3 3QS
+44 (0)20 7349 8829
www.felt-london.com
Mon–Sat 10–6pm

Fifi Wilson

'Effortlessly cool, creative clothes, for independent, hard-working, fun, busy women.' This is the mantra of Fi Lovett, owner of **Fifi Wilson**. Sounds too good to be true? Well, not really. Unless you haven't made it to her Chelsea outpost yet. Filled with designer clothes, accessories and jewellery, all items have a retro, nostalgic charm and include feminine and cute labels such as Manoush, Antoni Alison, Sonia Rykiel, Vivetta and Elizabeth Lau, among others. Fifi Wilson's strength lies in its laid back attitude. You are free to check out merchandise without being hassled by annoying members of staff, in an environment that is above all friendly and welcoming. All in all, this is a great shopping destination for original, trendy and utterly charming clothes. *DG*

MAP 13 Ref. 31
Fifi Wilson
1 Godfrey Street
Chelsea SW3 3TA
+44 (0)20 7352 3232
www.fifiwilson.com
Mon–Sat 10–6pm

Opium

As soon as you come near the shop, you feel as if you are about to enter a Buddhist temple: the air is filled with the exotic aroma of incense sticks. For **Opium** is a temple to the marvels of India. For over ten years, Terry Kitching has been trawling the Indian sub-continent, assembling unique treasures, which form the core of this amazing and thoroughly unique shop. Expect to find stone and wood temple pillars, palace doors from Rajasthan, colonial beds from Calcutta, stunning mirrors made from 18th century carved doorway frames, marble elephants from Udaipur as well as Hindu deities carved in marble from Varanasi. Opium also stocks more affordable offerings, such as door knobs made of colonial porcelain, old spice boxes as well as silk bed throws made by craftspeople in the villages of Rajasthan, Gujarat and Uttar Pradesh. *DG*

MAP 13 Ref. 34

Opium
414 Kings Road
Chelsea SW10 0LJ
+44 (0)20 7795 0700
www.opiumshop.co.uk
Mon–Sat 10–6.30pm
Sun 12–5pm

The Chelsea Teapot

Hot on the latest craze for all things traditional, **The Chelsea Teapot** is all about serving the best English afternoon tea with a slice of moist Victoria sponge cake, in a place that you feel as if time has stopped. Oozing old school charm, with yummy cupcake coloured walls, a stall full of glass stands featuring the best and most scrumptious cakes, scones and jelly beans and a group of friendly ladies behind the counter, you won't be able to resist. Did we mention that home-made gluten and wheat free cupcakes and sandwiches are on offer too? Here you can also find the cutest little accessories for serving the perfect 'tea' at home: from cupcake-inspired mugs to cute candles and funky cake and chocolate decorations. 'A little heaven' indeed. *DG*

MAP 13 Ref. 33
The Chelsea Teapot
402 Kings Road
Chelsea SW10 0LJ
+44 (0) 20 7751 5975
www.thechelseateapot.com
Tue–Fri 8.30–6.30pm
Sat 9.30–6.30pm
Sun 12–6.30pm

Dragons of Walton Street

When you enter this small establishment, you feel as if you have stepped into a Roald Dahl or Beatrix Potter fairytale. Beautifully made pieces of furniture and huge Victorian doll houses dominate the space, evoking a nostalgic kind of charm. **Dragons of Walton Street** is a family business from Sussex, starting out 30 years ago, when Rosie Fisher started commissioning hand-painted furniture for her children. Today it offers not just beautifully hand-painted bespoke furniture, but whole design ideas for imaginative children's bedrooms and playrooms; and it doesn't stop there. Details such as personalised hairbrushes with a favourite cartoon hero, union jack themed-beds and even miniature Louis XIV sofas featuring fairies are also on offer. It may not come cheap, yet every piece will be a memory that any child will cherish for life. *DG*

MAP 13 Ref. 27
Dragons of Walton Street
23 Walton Street
Knightsbridge SW3 2HX
+44 (0)20 7589 3795
www.dragonsofwaltonstreet.com
Mon–Fri 9.30–5.30pm
Sat 10–5pm

Few and Far

You may get the impression that you have just come to a glossy modern art gallery of the Saatchi calibre instead: all wide open spaces and quirky installations. But these are not Charles Saatchi's new 'Sensations' rather than Priscilla Carluccio's unique selection of designers and artisans. The ex-wife of restaurateur Antonio and sister of design impresario Terence Conran, Priscilla has accumulated some serious credentials over the years. After all, she was the driving force behind two lifestyle successes, The Conran Shop and Habitat. Recently, she has been putting all her energy into a new project; **Few and Far**, that is, a furniture and lifestyle store with a cosmopolitan view on design. Expect here the usual 'suspects', like furniture by Paola Navone or Cappelini but with a quirky detail thrown into the mix: a knit dress from the Faroe Islands, a stool brought over from India or a metal cantelabra from Senegal. *DG*

MAP 13 Ref. 25
Few and Far
242 Brompton Road
Chelsea SW3 2BB
+44 (0) 20 7225 7070
www.fewandfar.net
Mon–Sat 10 – 6pm
Sun 12–5pm

Percy Bass

It's small, dark, narrow and cavernous. It's overcrowded with heaps of objects that make you think this could be the refuge of an obsessive hoarder. Alas, it's not. **Percy Bass** is an interior design business, now run by Jane Morris, which has been in the same location in Knightsbridge for nearly a century. Morris' style is quintessentially British – quaint, idiosyncratic with a touch of eccentricity – but always with attention to detail. So, if you are looking for that camel-shaped doorstop (£36) or an ice bucket that looks like old leather books stacked together (£159) even coat hangers that have 'My beautiful Gown' sewn on them (£10), well, here is the place. You will also find an array of discounted fabrics and special gifts for special friends. Their cushions, embroidered with animals or witty sayings, such as 'I'm not 40. I'm 18 with 22 years experience' are definitely a must buy. *DG*

MAP 13 Ref. 26
Percy Bass
184 Walton Street
Knightsbridge SW3 2JL
+44 (0)20 7589 4853
www.percybass.com
Mon–Fri 9.30–6pm
Sat 10–6pm
Sun 1–5pm

A visit to **Venetia Studium** is like visiting the Victoria and Albert museum. It is not just atmospheric but also full of details on the history of fashion and textiles. After all Venetia Studium, not only produce the infamous Mariano Fortuny applique lanterns but also they make a whole range of interior design items, in Fortuny's great spirit with his East-meets-West style. You will be amazed by the richness and the colours of the precious and ethnic looking fabrics you will find here, such as Byzantine cushions, Ottoman and Chinese inspired table runners, rugs, tassels, bedcovers as well as beautiful silk and velvet scarves, all made in the label's Venetian workshops. Here one can even order or restore one of Fortuny's infamous pleated dresses, if you are lucky to own an original, that is. In an age of mass produced objects, Venetia Studium's concept is actually a blessing from the sky. *DG*

MAP 13 Ref. 28
Venetia Studium
37 Beauchamp Place
Knightsbridge SW3 1NU
+44 (0)20 72250110
www.venetiastudium.com
Mon–Sat 10.30–6pm

Anushka

Anushka is the retail outlet for a recent entry in the world of fashion, ethical luxury womenswear brand, Ekta. Meaning 'harmony' in Hindi, Ekta is all about a contemporary look with slightly bohemian details using traditional knitting techniques. The brand features soft lamb wool mix cardigans and knitted dresses, jersey tops in rich hues such as greys and berries but also a wide range of scarves and shawls made of Australian merino wool and in a variety of styles (jacquard, woven, embroidered). The label is designed in-house in London and manufactured in the Far East and India but the great thing is that all clothes are environmentally friendly. Not only are the materials used biodegradable but also all dyes are natural, with a range of prices that go across the board. The right mix, for sure. *DG*

MAP 14 Ref. 35
Anushka
281 New King's Road
Fulham SW6 4RE
+44 (0)20 7731 3255
www.ektalifestyle.co.uk
Mon–Sat 10–6pm

Samuel Chan is a Hong-Kong born, UK furniture design graduate that has carved a name in the design world for his organic style and his superb hand-finished furniture. His bright, zen-like showroom and studio, called **Channels** is testament to the spirit of this design genius, who created his first product, 'Rocking Chair' as a present to his mother, when he was just 15. Chan's impressive CV includes designing furniture for luxury hotels like the Lanesborough, and iconic furniture shops, like Heals the iconic furniture store as well as pieces for gallery shows. Chan's trademark style: natural materials such as wood which he explores in original, interesting and 'progressive' ways, showcasing an approach to design, which is all about 'less is more'. Among the shop's highlights are the 'motley drums', a series of furniture with multi-functional character (seats that can be used as tables and vice versa), which actually look like drums, all made from reclaimed and sustainable materials. *DG*

MAP 14 Ref. 37
Channels
1-3 New King's Road
Fulham SW6 4SB
+44 (0)20 7371 0301
www.channelsdesign.com
Mon–Sat 10–5.30pm

Deuxieme

Deuxieme abides perfectly by the adage 'One person's unwanted item is another's treasure'. This small shopping haunt specialises in second-hand fashion whether you are a buyer or a seller. Some of the items on sale include highly desirable names like Jimmy Choo, Frost French, Prada, Gucci but also top high street labels like LK Bennett as well as vintage pieces at really affordable prices; at a recent trip, for example we found a pink Luella cardigan for £39 and a Louis Vuitton bag for £75. Stock is renewed daily and is extensive: from shoes to beautiful art deco costume jewellery and accessories. You could literally spend hours in here; not only is there a cute garden cafe where you can take a fair-trade coffee break (clutching that Prada dress of course, you don't want someone else to get it) but also there is free wifi so you can stay updated on what's going on outside. *DG*

MAP 14 Ref. 34
Deuxieme
299 New King's Road
Fulham SW6 4RE
+44 (0)20 7736 3696
www.deuxieme.co.uk
Mon–Sat 10–6pm
Sun 11–5pm

Indian Summer

Blame it all on a trip to India. That's all it took Ruth Kehoe and her friend Karin Andreasson to recreate a second '**Indian Summer**' in 2004, a beautiful 'lifestyle' boutique whose actual vibe transports you to the casual and buzzy Indian bazaars. For a start, the pink exterior blows you away, as it prepares you for the vibrant and thoroughly feminine paradise that you will encounter inside. This includes not just clothes, but a quirky mix of homewares, jewellery, children's toys and beauty products, all sourced from upcoming and unique labels. Some of the perennial bestsellers include the ever popular mid-length cotton kaftans (£25), silk pashminas imported from India (59.95) imported from India, candles, cups, furniture, coin necklaces (£31), cute knitted berry hats (£17.95) and rattles (£10.50) for your little ones. Honestly, you won't be able to get out of there holding just one item. *DG*

MAP 14 Ref. 39
Indian Summer
624c Fulham Road
Fulham SW6 5RS
+44 (0)20 7731 8234
www.indiansummershop.com
Mon–Sat 10–6.30pm
Sun 12–5pm

Katie & Jo

Fed up with the routine of their daily jobs, longtime friends, Jo Thyne and Katie Broadbent decided to spice up their lives by doing their own thing. Having lived in Parsons Green for years, it was at a dinner when they came up with the idea for '**Katie & Jo**', a boutique with clothes and accessories that caters to the stylish needs of 30 to 45 year-old women (mothers and professionals alike). The concept is based on bringing feminine, contemporary brands from the US, Australia, France and Sweden, especially ones that are not widely available in London. Much of the selection also showcases their complimentary relationship: Broadbent is a fan of the 'Parisian chic', while Thyne likes clothes with an edgy touch. Among the 'treasures' you can find here, are art-nouveau inspired wedges from Cleo B, Sretsis easy going separates, Superfine jeans, bohemian Shakuhachi dresses and statement jewellery by Bex Rox. *DG*

MAP 14 Ref. 36
Katie & Jo
253 New King's Road
Fulham SW6 4RB
+44 (0)20 7736 5304
www.katieandjo.com
Mon–Wed 10–7pm
Thu 10–8pm Fri10–6pm
Sat–Sun 10–5pm

Sarah Mahaffy describes herself as one of retail's 'late bloomers'. After all, before she opened **Maharani**, back in 2006, she had carved a 27-year career in book publishing. As the name suggests (maharani is the wife of a maharajah, an Indian prince), her SW6 emporium specialises in a wide yet exclusive selection of clothes and accessories, like silk jackets, cashmere shawls, jewellery, home accessories (bedspreads and quilts) as well as antique textiles from the Indian sub-continent, especially from exotic places like Jaipur and Hyderabad. 'We aim to show our customers just some of the riches that are to be found there.' Mahaffy says. If you want to delve into Indian craftsmanship more, Maharani hold special events during the year, some of which include talks on textiles.

DG

MAP 14 Ref. 38

Maharani
26 Parsons Green Lane
Fulham SW6 4HS
+44 (0)20 7384 4538
www.maharanitrading.com
Mon–Fri 10–6.30pm
Wed 10–8pm
Sat 10–5pm

Profeet

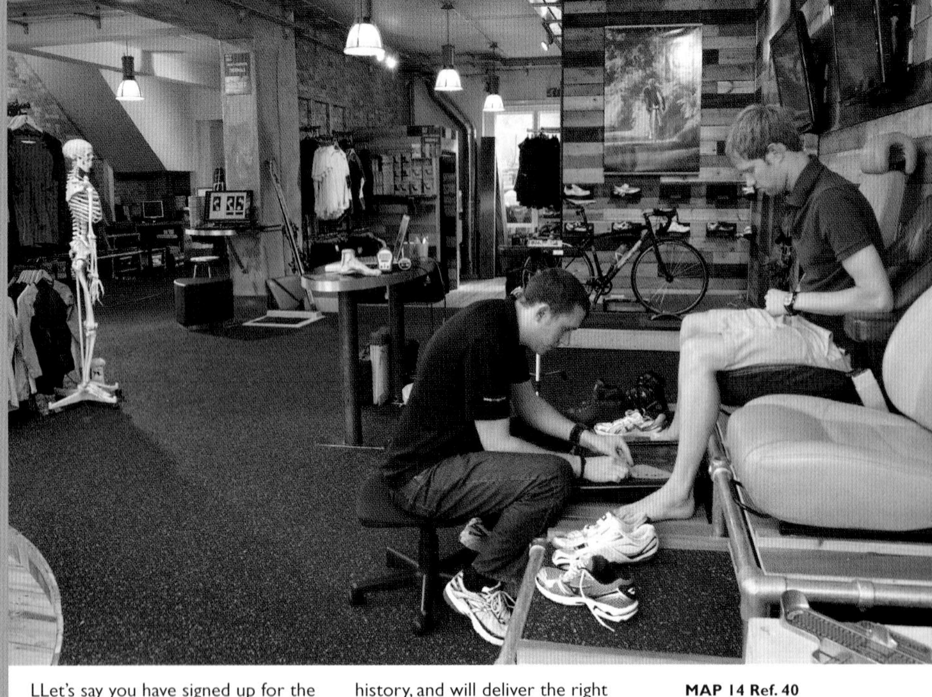

LLet's say you have signed up for the London marathon and you need a pair of running shoes but the sort of pair that doesn't give you blisters. Or the sort of pair, which minimises pain and increases your performance. 'Does it really exist,' you may ask. Well, it actually does. Just head to **Profeet**, London's premium makers of custom-made running shoes. Their personal advice service uses cutting edge technology which analyses your biomechanics, your activity, your movement as well as any injuries history, and will deliver the right solution: a pair of shoes specially designed for your needs. Profeet also provides the same service for many other adrenaline inducing sports, such as skiing, cycling and even climbing. The end result as attested by its loyal fans: more power transfer and comfort. No pain, no gain? That's now a myth. *DG*

MAP 14 Ref. 40
Profeet
867-869 Fulham Road
Fulham SW6 5HP
+44 (0)20 3411 9782
www.profeet.co.uk
Mon–Fri 10–6pm
Tue–Thu 10–8pm
Sat 9–6pm Sun 10–4pm

The Workshop (Page 226)

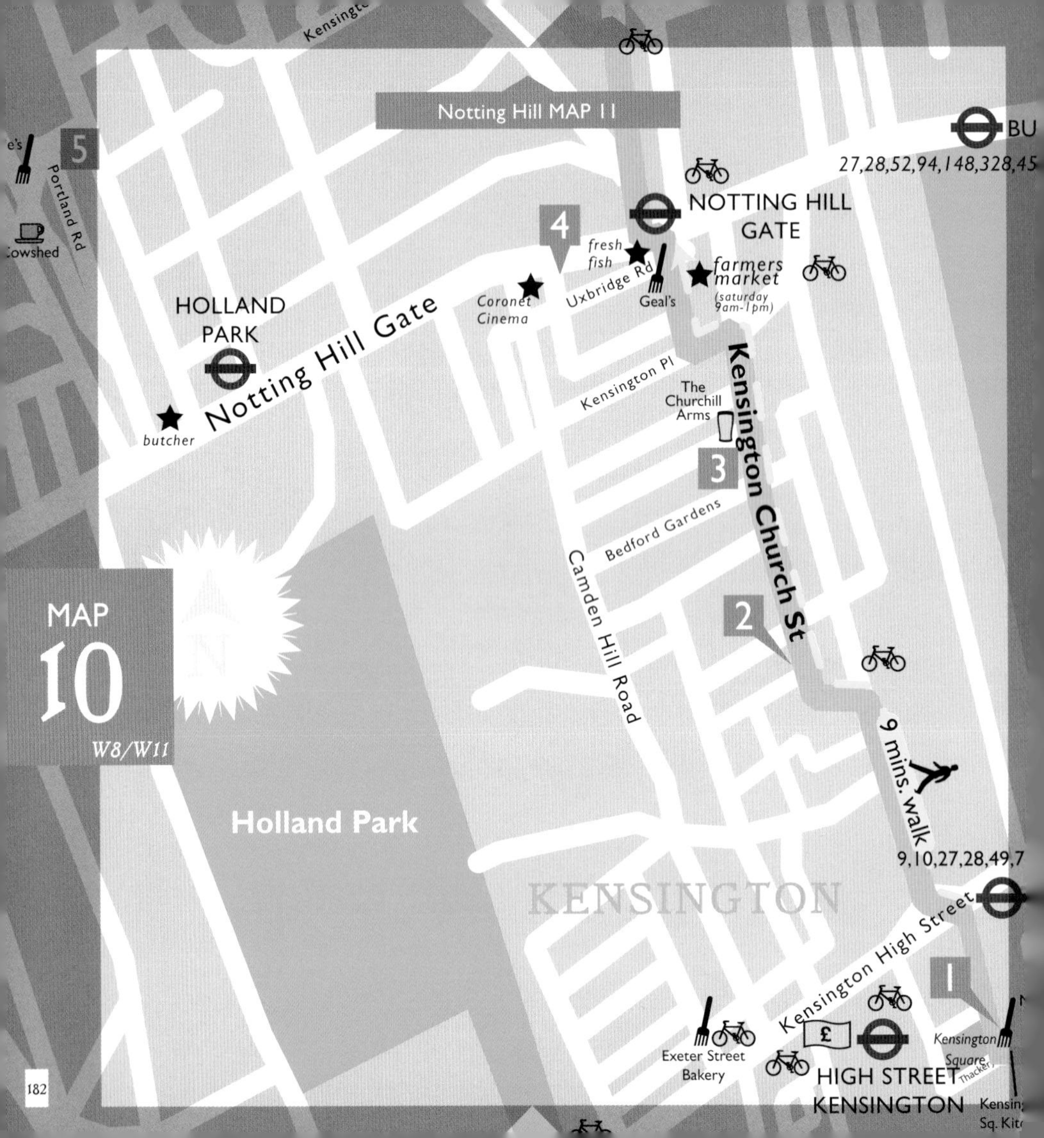
Kensingto
Notting Hill MAP 11
5
e's
Portland Rd
Cowshed
BU
27,28,52,94,148,328,45
NOTTING HILL GATE
4
fresh fish
Uxbridge Rd
Geal's
farmers market
(saturday 9am-1pm)
Coronet Cinema
HOLLAND PARK
Notting Hill Gate
butcher
Kensington Pl
The Churchill Arms
3
Kensington Church St
Bedford Gardens
Camden Hill Road
2
MAP
10
W8/W11
9 mins. walk
Holland Park
9,10,27,28,49,7
KENSINGTON
Kensington High Street
1
Kensington Square
Thackeray
Exeter Street Bakery
£
HIGH STREET KENSINGTON
Kensin
Sq. Kit

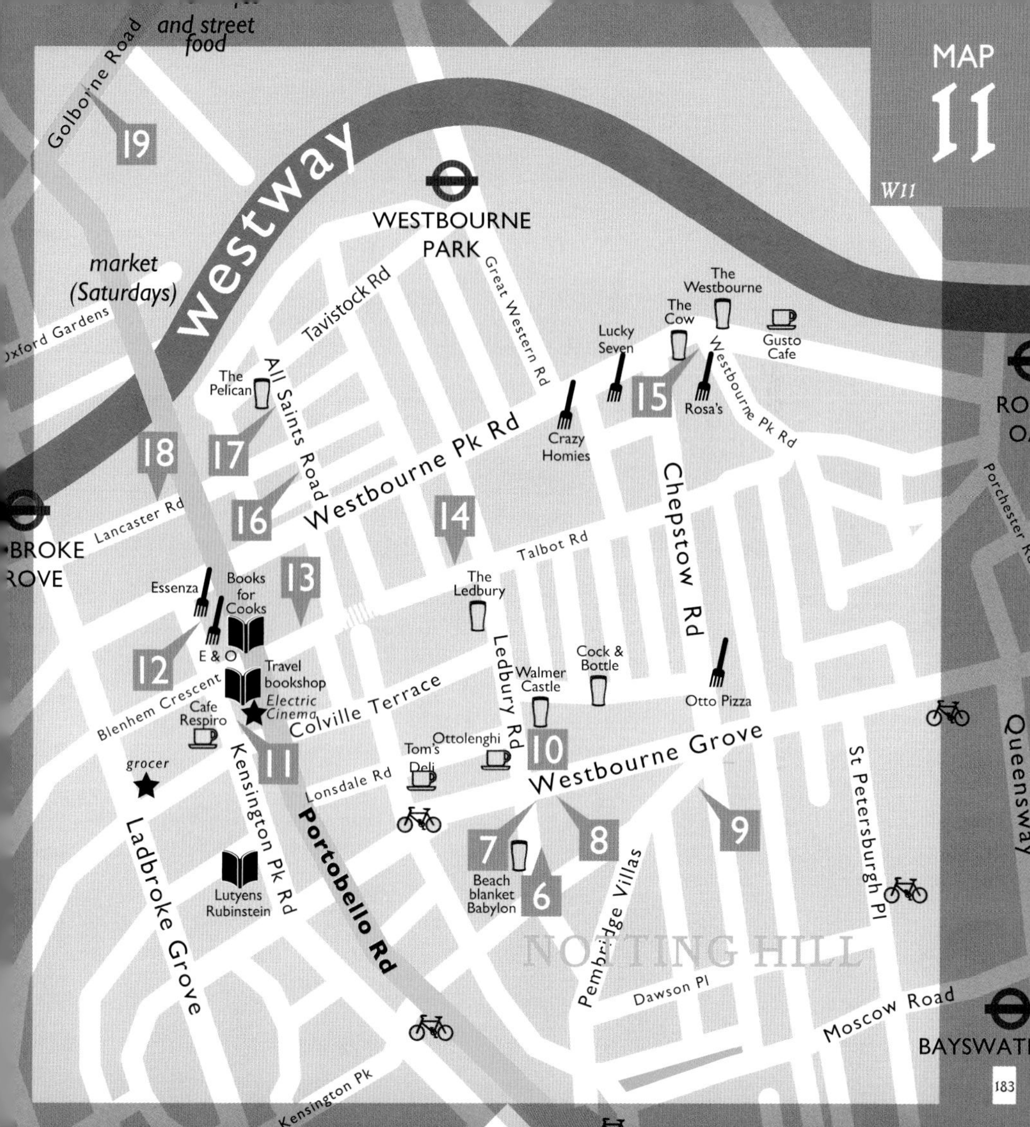
and street food
MAP
11
W11
Golborne Road
19
Westway
WESTBOURNE PARK
market (Saturdays)
Oxford Gardens
Tavistock Rd
Great Western Rd
All Saints Road
The Pelican
18
17
16
15
14
13
12
11
10
9
8
7
6
Lancaster Rd
Westbourne Pk Rd
The Westbourne
The Cow
Lucky Seven
Gusto Cafe
Rosa's
Crazy Homies
Westbourne Pk Rd
Porchester Rd
Chepstow Rd
Talbot Rd
The Ledbury
Ledbury Rd
Essenza
Books for Cooks
E & O
Travel bookshop
Electric Cinema
Blenheim Crescent
Cafe Respiro
Colville Terrace
Walmer Castle
Cock & Bottle
Otto Pizza
Ottolenghi
Tom's Deli
Westbourne Grove
St Petersburgh Pl
Queensway
grocer
Lonsdale Rd
Kensington Pk Rd
Portobello Rd
Ladbroke Grove
Lutyens Rubinstein
Beach blanket Babylon
Pembridge Villas
NOTTING HILL
Dawson Pl
Moscow Road
BAYSWATE
Kensington Pk
BROKE
ROVE
RO
O

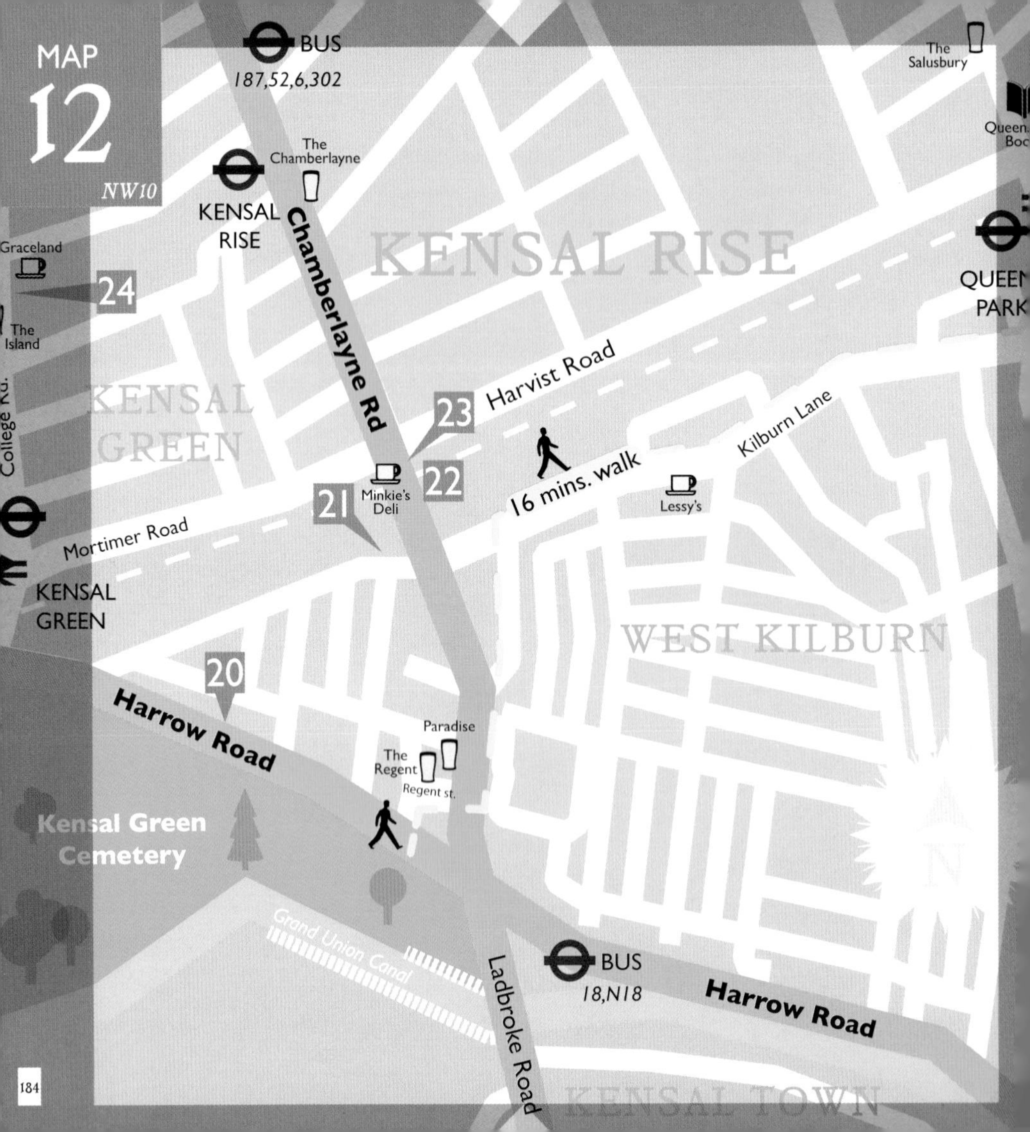
MAP
12
NW10
BUS
187,52,6,302
The Chamberlayne
KENSAL RISE
The Salusbury
KENSAL RISE
QUEEN PARK
Graceland
24
The Island
Chamberlayne Rd
Harvist Road
23
Kilburn Lane
KENSAL GREEN
College Rd.
Minkie's Deli
22
21
16 mins. walk
Lessy's
Mortimer Road
KENSAL GREEN
WEST KILBURN
20
Harrow Road
Paradise
The Regent
Regent st.
Kensal Green Cemetery
Grand Union Canal
Ladbroke Road
BUS
18,N18
Harrow Road
KENSAL TOWN

MAP
13
SW5/SW£
Harrods
KNIGHTSBRIDGE
Queen's Gate
BUS
49,74
Science Museum
Natural History Museum
Cromwell Road
Brompton Quarter Cafe
Merchant's Yard
Beauchamp Pl
Pont Street
Cadogan Square
25
28
27
26
Walton Street
The Enterprise
Farmers Market
(Saturday 9am-2pm)
La Brasserie
Brompton Road
Jack's
Admiral Codrington
Harrington Gardens
SOUTH KENSINGTON
SLOANE SQUARE
Draycott Ave
Sloane Ave
Whiteheads Grove
Draycott Pl
Old Brompton Rd
Gloucester Road
Elystan St
Saatchi Gallery
Chelsea Bridge
grocer
Album
29
Royal Marsden Hospital
BUS
430,C1
Cale Street
BUS
11,19,22,211
30
Sydney Street
31
Markham
CHELSEA
Fulham Road
Old Church St
The Trafalgar
Kings Rd
Belocq
23 mins. walk
The Phene
Oakley St
32
Park walk
8 over 8
Buonasera
Love Cake
Chelsea Embankment
33
34
Beaufort St
Albert Bridge
Kings Rd
Battersea Park

MAP
14
SW6
BUS
14,414
Clonmel Road
Lilyville Road
Elmstone Road
39
Radipole Road
Local Hero
Fulham Road
Epple Road
Purser's Cross Rd.
Chesilton Road
38
Parsons Green Lane
Novello Street
Mimosa Street
10 mins. walk
PARSONS GREEN
Ackmar Road
PARSONS GREEN
White Horse
40
Parsons Green
Munster Road
St. Dionis Street
Parsons Green
Parsons Green
Eddiscombe Road
Guion Road
36
New King's Road
35
34
Broomhouse
BUS
22,424
(di'zain)

Columbia Market traders (Map 4 Page 78)

La Petite Poissonerie Primrose Hill (Page 211)

N1 *Islington*
N1 *Angel*
EC1 *Exmouth Market*
NW1 *Primrose Hill*
N10 *Muswell Hill*
N10 *Crouch End*
N16 *Stoke Newington*
N16 *Newington Green*

Nic Rascle, a trained chef, likes to stay close and personal to his latest catch. **La Petite Poissonerie** has taken the art of fish to new heights.

Aria

This song to contemporary design is housed in the erstwhile Barnsbury Hall, a lofty space of many levels. Beautifully converted from an 1850s music and meeting hall, it' s notable for being the venue that saw a young Michael Collins sworn into the Irish Republican Brotherhood. Today, a spirit of patriotism infuses the choice of home-grown products at **Aria**. Alongside the ubiquitous Euro contenders Starck, Kartell, Alessi et al, British design and manufacture is strongly represented by Anthony Dickens, Black + Blum, Barber Osgerby, Owen Barry, John Smedley, Vivienne Westwood, Adam Aaronson, Lush Designs, Highland Tweeds, Tweedmill and others. Recipe books are from the revered taste buds at Moro, The Eagle and Leon. There's lighting, homewares, gifts and furniture. Jewellery has a shelf of its own, literally a mezzanine above the main floor. Staff are likely to be moonlighting designers and are wonderfully knowledgeable about the products. *GT*

MAP 16 Ref. 16
Aria
Barnsbury Hall
Barnsbury Street
Islington N1 1PN
+44 (0)20 7704 6222
www.ariashop.co.uk
Mon–Fri 10–6.30pm
Sun 10–6.30pm
Sun 12–6pm

For those who are resolute that the quintessential metropolitan look can only be achieved in a shade of black, boutique **Cop-Copine** is the dark crest of perfection. With two shops on Upper Street, No.110 offers a gentle introduction for the first timer. It's at No.184 where the influence of Japanese assymetry and avant-garde shapes is more noticeable and for which the faithful return. The French, Catalan, Greek and Brazilian girls who've made London their home are at the top of that list. If their style is distinct from the indigenous it may have a lot to do with this shop. While Cop-Copine isn't exactly independent, each store in this loose chain has its own look and collection. Manufactured to high standards in Europe, innovative eco-textiles such as lyocell make a frequent appearance. On the shop floor, big changing rooms and well-placed mirrors show a confidence in their product that's entirely justifiable. *GT*

MAP 16 Ref. 14
Cop Copine
184 Upper Street
Islington N1 1RQ
+44 (0)20 7354 0012
www.cop-copine.com
Mon–Sat 10–6.30pm
Sun 12–6pm

Labour of Love

Look for the gold lettering of 193 Berwick above the door and you've found it. **Labour of Love**, that is, who stuck with the original Victorian signage because it was so damn lovely. And that sets the tone for everything else, from the wonky doorway and mosaic entrance to the quirky clothes and off-beat accessories, stocked solely on the basis of loveliness rather than a slavish need to conform to some didactic trend forecast. The buying bias is on a scale of chic to Dada, shown in their early championing of knitwear labels such as Kind and Yang Du and a fondness for colour and strong prints as manifest in the likes of Manish Arora, Ashish and Miriam Ocariz. Such gorgeous and well-made pieces have a longevity of style that will last seasons and team well with Labour of Love's own label shoes and accessories, exclusive to their shop and website. *GT*

MAP 16 Ref. 18
Labour of Love
193 Upper Street
Islington N1 2RQ
+44 (0)20 7354 9333
www.labour-of-love.co.uk
Mon–Fri 11–6.30pm
Sat 10.30–6.30pm
Sun 12–5.30pm

-10%
*Discount**

The Make Lounge

For the busy and impatient aspiring crafter, **The Make Lounge** has a solution. Create a silver filigree ring, a fascinator or a bag in just one class! Too good to be true? Better believe it. Master your sewing machine by way of making an apron. Find your way around the overlocker to perfect a stretch t-shirt. Screen-print a tea-towel, bind a book, alter your jeans: all in an evening. No need to sign up for the usual term of classes that you know you'll never attend. Better still, rather than a cold classroom or church hall, sessions are held in the purpose-designed comfort of The Make Lounge with sustaining snacks and drinks to fuel the creative fire. It's a super sociable space and the adjacent shop has all the bits you need to continue making at home, along with inspiring books to keep that new-found talent burning. *GT*

MAP 16 Ref. 17

The Make Lounge
49-51 Barnsbury Street
Islington N1 1TP
+44 (0)20 7609 0275
www.themakelounge.com

Mosquito Bikes

The folk at **Mosquito** are wide-eyed at the ever-increasing mass of cyclists powering past their door on Essex Road. When they opened over 25 years ago everyone was known to them at least by sight and the community was clubby. Having grown up with the trend, their wealth of cycle know-how is vast and cyclists new, weary, muddy or fast will all find their service and range of bikes hard to beat. Mosquito also has two qualified Serotta Bike Fit Technicians available for SizeCycle assessments. Whether you're spending thousands on a bike or just hours in the saddle this 2 hour analysis ensures injury-free cycling by adjusting the geometry of a bike to match your individual size and style of movement. As standard, this comes free with the purchase of a more expensive bike but a session can also be booked to fit and correct an existing bike that's causing problems. *GT*

MAP 16 Ref. 13
Mosquito Bikes
123 Essex Road
Islington N1 2SN
+44 (0)20 7226 8765
www.mosquito-bikes.co.uk
Mon–Fri 8.30–7pm
Sat 10–6pm

Ottolenghi

At this flagship restaurant the line of conviviality extends from the seated diners at the long communal tables through the elegant tasters perched at the bar to the waves of customers rolling up to take away from the most sumptuously laden counter in North London. The proof is in the variety of the converted: a couple in their 80s enjoying a pre-theatre supper, girls from the office sharing mezze plates, a bloke in jeans, men in dark suits, family groups. At the tables outside, laughing mothers with smiling babies eat cake and from the other side of the road a woman dices with a speeding police car, her eyes only for **Ottolenghi** and its luscious tarts. Everyone loves this place with its noisy Mediterranean flavours. The secret's already out. All that's to add is the lesser known fact that on Upper Street they take bookings for dinner. So relax. *GT*

MAP 16 Ref. 15
Ottolenghi
287 Upper Street
Islington N1 2TZ
+44 (0)20 7288 1454
www.ottolenghi.co.uk
Mon–Sat 8–11pm
Sun 9–7pm

Palette

If you're still wistful for that early Gaultier parka, circa 1980, or have long yearned for a statement piece from the '70s, perhaps a Janice Wainwright jacket or a Bill Gibb show-stopper in braided silk embroidered leather then your nirvana is **Palette**. Discerning and picky? Welcome home! There's no rummaging required here. Items are well displayed and clearly marked, if not quite with provenance, then comprehensively with dates and materials. Of immaculate museum quality, they're treated with due respect. Contemporary chic fills the remaining rails: future classics from Eugene Lin, Anna Aichinger, Aganovich and the infernally interesting Rundholz slide easily alongside "modern vintage" Dior, Givenchy and the kooky Koos van den Akker. While you're in the museum mode of mind, why not make it an afternoon of aesthetics and visit the Estorick, just a fashionable stroll across the Square. *GT*

MAP 16 Ref. 20
Palette
21 Canonbury Lane
Islington N1 2AS
+44 (0)20 7288 7428
www.palette-london.com

At **The Sampler**, first and foremost, one samples. This way you get the good stuff, that is, the stuff that you like. Rather than the stuff with the pretty label, or the bottle on promotion. The point being that taste is a personal thing. It's fine to take advice, even from the man in the shop, but ultimately the best wine is chosen by you. So top up a card and get slurping. Everyone else is. Afternoons here aren't dissimilar to a party and it's good to work the room. With over 1500 hand-picked wines on offer and a fortnightly rotation of 80 in the machines ready to sample at any one time it'll be a while before boredom hits. Should direction be called for, staff are knowledgeable and can confidently chart a course through the rare vintages, unusual places of origin and little-known vineyards. *GT*

MAP 16 Ref. 19
The Sampler
266 Upper Street
Islington N1 2UQ
+44 (0)20 7226 9500
www.thesampler.co.uk
Mon–Sat 11.30–9pm
Sun 11.30–7pm

Fat Faced Cat

They don't make retro like they used to. At **Fat Faced Cat** the perfumed air is redolent of a private members club or chi-chi boutique. And the scene set is worthy of a Merchant Ivory film with leather luggage, wartime ephemera and gentlemen's sports accessories dressing the windows. 'Upscale vintage' is their stock, claim the owners and they carry the couture names to back it up. Despite this, they're not slaves to labels. There's nothing to stop an M&S handbag turning up on the rails if the look and quality is right. The range is Victorian to 1980s and might include a mid '70s maxi-dress from Hawaii, a hand-stitched cashmere jacket by Cardin or a 1950s blonde mink cape, all hand-picked by the owners at antique and vintage fairs. Should explain why the fashion industry have already sniffed it out. *GT*

MAP 16 Ref. 12
Fat Faced Cat
22-24 Camden Passage
Islington N1 8ED
+44 (0)20 7354 0777
Mon, Tue, Thu 11–7pm
Wed 9–6pm
Fri–Sat 10–6pm
Sun 12–6pm

Jacqueline Byrne

"You made me feel beautiful" reads a handwritten card. "You're a genius" states another. What better recommendation than the testimonials of **Jacqueline Byrne**'s clients. This designer, whose skill keeps her in demand with some members of the Royal family among others, creates handmade wedding dresses using traditional construction techniques. Vintage-inspired and romantic as a Waterhouse painting, all are cut to fit and flatter, sylphs and tomboys alike. Fabrics include layers of silk tulle and authentic French lace. Beading, hand-sewn in London, is custom-designed. Prices can vie with some ready-to-wear dresses yet these charcoal-sketched designs are unique and crafted by hand, right down to the hand-stitched hem. Over 3 months, through consultations, fittings and many cups of tea, a bride is made. Jacqueline's insistence that the feel of the dress on the wearer's skin is as valuable as its visual impact is borne out by those piles of thank-you cards. *GT*

MAP 15 Ref. 2

Jacqueline Byrne
18 Arlington Way
Islington EC1R 1UY
+44 (0)20 7278 7014
www.jacquelinebyrne.co.uk
(By appointment only)

Lie down i think i love you

Charming and eccentric, this quiet shop on genteel Georgian Amwell Street might have been here for a long long time. Daylight creeps through the silk scarves in the window to reveal fabric patching on the care-worn floorboards. Shoes, bags and accessories are presented in cabinets that belong to another era. Those romantic souls who hanker for tactile engagement with a more feminine age will love the soft leather bags that are the mainstay of **Lie down i think i love you**. Selling as a label since 2006, the shop came into being in 2009 to allow the designers to offer their product in a much more personal fashion. Clients are invited to consult with them to create a bespoke bag, choosing a vintage scarf from the designers' hand-picked selection to co-ordinate with their preferred shade of leather. Beautiful print shoes and sweet dresses can also be bought in-store. *GT*

MAP 15 Ref. 4
Lie down i think i love you
33 Amwell Street
Islington EC1R 1UR
+44 (0)20 7833 1100
www.liedownithinkiloveyou.com
Mon–Fri 10–6pm

It's not just knitters who respond to the warmth, colour and softness of the yarns at **Loop**. With the variety numbering over 100, from all around the globe, it's boggling to behold the 8ply Mongolian cashmere, organic merino, Peruvian alpaca, Japanese bamboo yarn, silk, llama fibre and the many possibilities of cotton. More uncommon blends such as silk covered steel will specifically appeal to weavers and jewellery makers. Divided across a wall of cubby holes, the skeins form a kaleidescopic backdrop to the upstairs lounge which is arranged with easy chairs for anyone wishing to drop in with their knitting. This is where they hold the great SOS sessions, with tea and cake, for help with those tricky stitches, as well as a plethora of other classes. Late night openings allow for leisurely perusal of textile themed gifts such as textured ceramics, jewellery and mixed media artwork. *GT*

MAP 16 Ref. 10
Loop
15 Camden Passage
Islington N1 8EA
+44 (0)20 7288 1160
www.loopknitting.com
Tue–Sat 11–6pm
except Thu 11–7.30pm
Sun 12–5pm

My Sugarland

When you're sick of trawling the internet for all the different things that comprise today's wardrobe and need to engage with a real shop again, where do you go? Still short of time, who might have all those elements you require – new, vintage, accessories and jewellery – in one place? **My Sugarland** is run by stylist Zoe Lem. With years of experience dressing people in the public eye she applies her well-honed sense to every item in this collection. The newest and most interesting designers are showcased here, alongside hand-picked luxury vintage including a large bridal section featuring Victorian through to 1960s dresses. All staff are stylists in their own right and are on hand to offer advice. This extends to personal wardrobe analysis, possibly re-working existing items for a new look. The shop is spacious, comfortable and infinitely inspiring. *GT*

MAP 15 Ref. 1
My Sugarland
402-404 St. John Street
Islington EC1V 4NJ
+44 (0)20 7841 7131
www.mysugarland.co.uk
Sun–Mon 12–6pm
Tue–Wed 11–6pm
Thu–Fri 11–7pm
Sat 10.30–6.30pm

Pigment & Patina

For urban romantics who dream of a parallel life in the country, Nicolas and Stefano of **Pigment & Patina** can manifest the vision. Specialists in French country furniture from the 18th and 19th centuries, specifically from the south-west regions, their shop is crammed with antique treats. Many things can be easily carried away for an immediate rustic touch in a contemporary home: linen tablecloths and hemp bedsheets, heavily wrought coat hooks and glazed farmhouse salting jars. But it's the large furniture, armoires and the like, often sourced at clients' request, that are the substance. Working with an expert restorer and artist, they repair and sometimes adapt these pieces to meet modern needs. Drawing on their own parallel lives as interior designers, they can also offer the full service required to recreate an entire look, paying particular attention to patinated finishes on walls, floors and ceilings. *GT*

MAP 15 Ref. 3

Pigment & Patina
48 Amwell Street
Islington EC1R 1XS
+44 (0)20 7833 0650
www.pigmentandpatina.com
Tue–Sat 10–6pm

*Discount**

Smug

Smug is probably how you'd feel if you lived in this dinky duplex. With its raised ground floor window overlooking Camden Passage, this lifestyle shop feels more like a comfortable apartment than a centre of commerce. The kitchen-themed area downstairs and upper level reception room have on offer everything required to kit out a bijou home almost entirely, albeit one that displays a taste for formica bordering on the fetishistic. From retro furniture, through illustrated cushions and vibrant kitchen utensils to cute jewellery and the make-up on your dressing table, it's all been thought of. Visitors with a taste for life's finer things will notice the original artwork throughout. Selected by the people behind the Lodeveans Collection, whose influence was instrumental in bringing the works of Tracey Emin et al to public acclaim, unique pieces cost between £200 and £500. A modest sum for your first share of the contemporary art market. *GT*

MAP 16 Ref. 9
Smug
13 Camden Passage
Islington N1 8EA
+44 (0)20 7354 0253
www.ifeelsmug.com
Wed, Fri, Sat 11–6pm
Thu 12–7pm
Sun 12–5pm

Looking much as it would have over a century ago when it first opened as a dairy, **Unpackaged** now operates in a style that's at once antique and the way of the future. Doing exactly as it would say on the tin, all goods sold here come loose. So if you're the customer who rips off the packaging in anger at the checkout then this is your spiritual supermarket. Any container is a good container and whether you want to fill your boots, a bike pannier or a spotted hanky, anything goes so long as it fits on the weighing scales.

Even yesterday's lunch box can be washed at Unpackaged's lovely sink in advance of a refill. Owner Catherine and her staff are joyously evangelical about reducing waste and the shop is a sensual pleasure smelling of fruit, leaves and dried goods. To change the world, no purchase is too small. *GT*

MAP 15 Ref. 6
Unpackaged
42 Amwell Street
Islington EC1R 1XT
+44 (0)20 7713 8368
www.beunpackaged.com
Mon–Fri 10–7pm
Sat 9–6pm

Wallace & Sewell

A working textile design studio, this tiny shop on a corner of Amwell Street is merely the tip of an iceberg. Downstairs, beneath the pavement, is where **Wallace Sewell** create woven designs that sell throughout the world. In the UK they can be found in shops at Tate and the British Museum as well as fashion stores. Their style is distinctive in its bold use of colour with geometric patterns worked out in wool, silk, cashmere, linen and cotton chenille. Designs available here include throws, cushions and scarves that haven't been produced for wholesale as well as pieces from earlier collections. Scarves are typically produced in runs of 25 to 50 making them fairly exclusive at prices between £40 and £140. Far more ubiquitous are their upholstery designs. From 2011 the London Tube's Central line seats will also be the proud bearers of the Wallace Sewell style. *GT*

MAP 15 Ref. 5
Wallace & Sewell
24 Lloyd Baker Street
Islington WC1X 9AZ
+44 (0)20 7833 2995
www.wallacesewell.com
Tue–Fri 10.30–5.30pm
Sat 11–6pm

Workshop

The deluxe ambiance of this particular **Workshop** could be misconstrued. Witness the early customers to Islington's latest fashion house who discovered to their delight that Italian quality can deliver a far lighter blow to the purse than expected. The concept at Workshop is as simple as its designs. To offer an enduring Italian elegance to London. Their range of unstructured dresses, coats and jackets in a signature fabric of boiled wool knitwear that has the semblance of felt is definitely not mass market. Designed by a London-based Italian and produced in Italy these are highly covetable garments to flatter an age range of twenty-five and beyond. Colours are muted and the silhouettes serene. Although predominantly for women, Workshop also produces men's wool jackets in the same well-tailored fashion. *GT*

MAP 16 Ref. 11
Workshop
19 Camden Passage
Islington N1 8EA
+44 (0)20 7226 3141
www.workshop-london.com
Mon–Sun 11–7pm

Bagman & Robin

Bagman and Robin a.k.a. Marco and Lee design highly individual leather and fabric bags. This dynamic duo operate out of a tiny atelier, at the back of an equally dinky shop where they also sell Lee's paintings and prints – roosters and goldfish being an enduringly colourful theme. The bags are a mix of svelte evening clutches and capacious day bags. Marco trained as mechanical engineer, specialising in thermo-dynamics. While his bags won't make you go faster, they've been engineered to last and are finely-turned with loving attention to detail. Working from a palette of matt and glossy leathers with embossed sections and incorporating fabric from vintage Italian fashion or Japanese kimonos each bag is practically unique with no more than 3 likely to be made in any one fabric and less than 15 in any particular style. Large day bags cost between £150 and £180 with the more petite starting at £40. *GT*

MAP 15 Ref. 7
Bagman & Robin
47 Exmouth Market
Islington EC1R 4QL
+44 (0)20 7833 8780
www.bagmanandrobin.com
Mon–Sat 11–6pm

The Klinik

Aptly located at the turn into Spa Fields is **the klinik** hairdressing salon. While clinically white in appearance, any sense of austerity is melted by the warmth of the welcome from this international team of stylists. Helmed by Swedish owner Anna there's no salon hierarchy, everyone here being equally qualified and performing the same tasks. This, along with the neutral and unintimidating interior, might explain why nearly half the client base is men. Or is it something to do with those cameras? A monitor at each seat allows the customer to see precisely what's happening to their locks. Designed to empower the patron, it's a mesmerising tool. Ever forward-looking, new products at the klinik include the sulphate, paraben and gluten-free *Unite* range, 100% ammonia-free colours by *L'Oréal* and a non-permanent Brazilian keratin treatment for smoothing frizzy hair that lasts for up to 4 months. *GT*

MAP 15 Ref. 8

The Klinik
28 Exmouth Market
Islington EC1R 4QE
+44 (0)20 7837 3771
www.theklinik.com
Mon–Fri 9–8pm
Sat 9–5pm

Judith Michael & Daughter

Its air thick with Wild Fig and Grape (courtesy of the shop's own candles), **Judith Michael & Daughter** is a vintage treasure trove offering shiny campness as well as retro cool. Mirrored Art Deco furniture and costume jewellery (including some made for the Suffragettes) keep the magpies happy, while 1950s Playboy magazines, Japanese fortune-telling cups and Brazilian voodoo dolls satisfy more quirky gift-buyers. Owner Gillian Anderson Price is one of the interiors experts on ITV's House Gift, and her keen eye sets the shop apart from identikit emporiums. The old is sprinkled with the new: Keep Calm And Carry On signs fit right in with vintage Union Jack cushions; Victorian Champagne saucers are accompanied by 'Harlequin' cutlery. Boasts Jude Law, Sadie Frost and Kate Moss as clients – but then so do most of our other Primrose Hill picks. *FM*

MAP 17 Ref. 21

Judith Michael & Daughter
73 Regents Park Road
Primrose Hill NW1 8UY
+44 (0)20 7722 9000
www.judithmichael.com
Mon–Sat 10–6pm
Sun 12–6pm

La Petite Poissonerie

Its shelves heaving with wasabi, pickled ginger and wakame and its floor taken up by a rowing boat filled with ice and the latest catch, **La Petite Poissonerie** is not your average fishmonger. French owner Nic Rascle, a trained chef, is so keen to espouse the wonders of gilled creatures that he's building a swanky kitchen downstairs to host classes ranging from sushi-making and filleting to longer sessions taking in lobster and foie gras (prices will start at £35 per person). 'I hope to create a lunchtime hour where people can come and learn a few dishes – such as moules marinieres, Thai and Spanish mussels cooked by competing teams – and then eat them with some wine,' he says, excitedly describing the herb garden he's planning to plant outside, with rosemary, thyme and lavender. Customers can wander around the boat to pick their fish of the day, or even take home some sushi-grade wares to eat raw. *FM*

MAP 17 Ref. 23

La Petite Poissonerie
75 Gloucester Avenue
Primrose Hill NW1 8LD
+44 (0)20 7483 4435
www.lapetitepoissonerie.com
Tues–Sat 9.30–7.30pm
Sun 10.30–5.30pm

Primrose Bakery

Primrose Hill could lay claim to being one of London's most fervent defenders of independents, as residents successfully blocked a Starbucks eight years ago, the first time the chain had been forced to back down. **Primrose Bakery** couldn't be further from the ubiquitous coffee purveyor, offering a warm, icing sugar-scented haven for locals and tourists to sit for hours. So popular that it attracts a queue worthy of a late-night kebab shop, synonymous with the recent cupcake revival (its first recipe book was a bestseller, and a second book is due out next year). After baking cupcakes for their children's birthday parties, two local mothers began supplying to deli Melrose and Morgan in 2004. They now supply Selfridges, Liberty and Fortnum & Mason, and a second Primrose Bakery opened in Covent Garden 18 months ago. The original has a reassuringly homemade feel, bunting and 1950s chairs offering a cosy setting for customers wanting tea and crumpets as well as cupcakes with flavours such as Earl Grey, peanut butter, rose and coconut. *FM*

MAP 17 Ref. 24
Primrose Bakery
69 Gloucester Avenue
Primrose Hill NW1 8LD
+44 (0)20 7483 4222
www.primrosebakery.org.uk
Mon–Sat 8.30–6pm
Sun 10–5pm

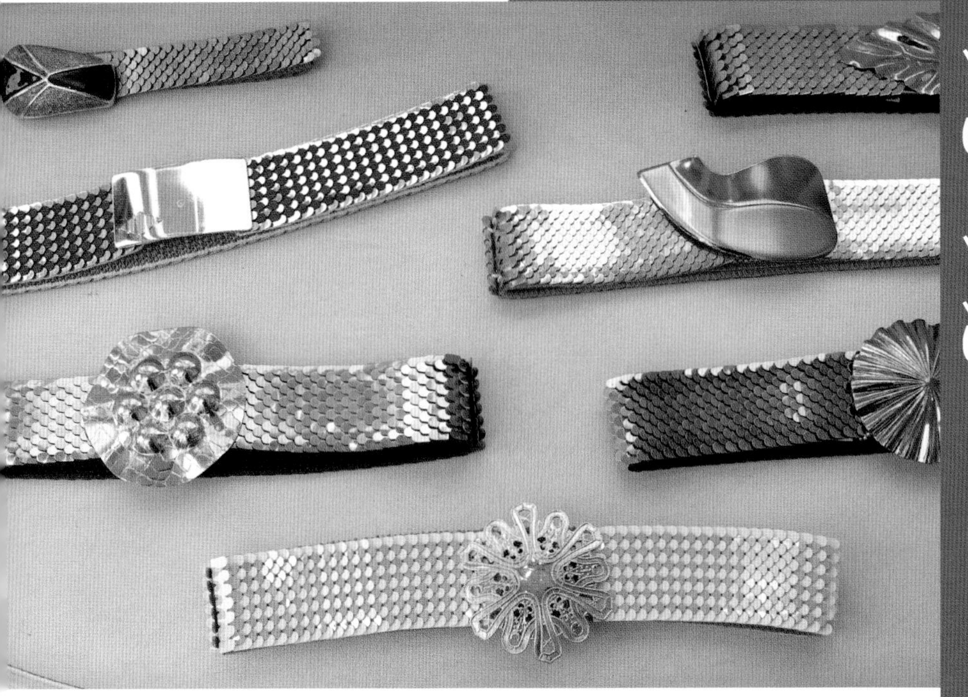

Shika Suki

Set up in 2004 by Central St Martins graduate Rachel Ducker, **Shika Suki** is more museum than shop. Every item has been lovingly tagged and arranged in a way that is curated rather than merely displayed, from the selection of vintage bisque Nancy Ann dolls in the corner to the wall of chiffon squares and silk scarves. Japan meets Portobello with Technicolor childrens' accessories, including vintage Dream Pets and Barbie cases, alongside shelves of neatly placed metal belts and owl necklaces. Quotes from Alice Temperley and Matthew Williamson on the shop's website attest to its fashion credentials, confirmed by a collection of Ossie Clark dresses. But it's the racks downstairs that set it apart: colour-coordinated cocktail dresses, beaded cardigans and bucket bags provide the range of Rokit without the feeling of ploughing through a car boot sale. *FM*

MAP 17 Ref. 25

Shika Suki
67 Gloucester Avenue
Primrose Hill NW1 8LD
+44 (0)20 7722 4442
www.shikasuki.com
Mon–Sun 11–7pm

Studio 8

The best independent shops have their own smells, and **Studio 8**'s scent speaks of old leather and the finer things in life. There's plenty of that for sale here – Italian label Calabrese's Pantcuoi slippers, with leather uppers and crepe soles, mingle with Barbour jackets and vintage watches (owner Simon Savage has just started selling these online, his passion for them inspired by his deep-sea diver father). Yet luxury brands mix with edgier designers to create a style that's a little bit Bond Street, a little bit Brick Lane. So a two-grand Heuer is joined by Timex multicoloured digital watches at £25 a pop, and Comme des Garcons loafers sit alongside £39 tennis shoes by Supergra. Womens labels include Acne, Ash and Rick Owens, and staff are so attentive they keep aside items they think regulars might like. A definite one-off. *FD*

MAP 17 Ref. 22
Studio 8
83 Regents Park Road
Primrose Hill NW1 8UY
+44 (0)20 7449 0616
www.studio8shop.com
Mon–Sat 10–6pm
Except Thu 10–7pm
Sun 12–5pm

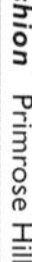

Bones

Like a delightfully disordered jewellery box, **Bones** is stuffed to the gills with things to adorn, embellish and tickle. Ceilings sparkle with candelabras, Moorish lamps and winking fairy lights while dressers groan with mirrors, frames and ceramics. Stock is modern-to-look vintage and rummaging is thoroughly recommended. Once the eye stills there are some quite solid furniture pieces anchoring the stock – large wooden chests with good tongue and groove joining – and Bones can order in larger items from their collection of catalogues. Quirky home-ware accessories are what they are beloved for, like a recession-friendly PIP china set starting from £9.50 (pastel palette, oriental print). The staff know their market and their clients and are impassioned members of the Traders Association, championing Independent shops' right, nay, duty to be different. Of which Bones is an eloquent, eccentric ambassador. *TT*

MAP 19 Ref. 31

Bones
253 Muswell Hill Broadway
Muswell Hill N10 1DE
+44 (0)20 8883 4730
www.bonesfurniture.co.uk
Mon–Sat 9.30–6pm
Sun 12–5pm

*Discount on items over £50**

Cha-Cha-Cha

Cha-Cha-Cha puts the eek! into weekend. School girls exclaim over Christian Dior sunglasses from the 70s (£65) and buyers from Hennes and Accessorize come to copy designs for their lines. There is not a bum note among the stock but the real find are the staff, sartorially passionate and with an encyclopaedic knowledge of their (four) rails. Use them. With their help we paired a red carpet, black vintage silk gown with hooks and eyes and a bustle (£100) with a 40s-ration inspired bolero jacket (£45) for less than the price of a Pringles skirt. Brides can beat the recession (£25 wedding dress) and old dresses need never die (Megan Stevenson upcycles old curtains/vintage dress material for her bespoke lampshades). Online there is furniture too but the real alchemy is in the attic to 30s jive and playful encouragement. *TT*

MAP 19 Ref. 32
Cha-Cha-Cha
20-22 Avenue Mews
Muswell Hill N10 3NP
+44 (0)773951 7855
+44 (0)7974 043616
www.cha-cha-cha.co.uk
Fri–Sat 11–5pm
Sun 12–5pm

Everything in **Cosi** speaks of impossibly good taste. From the minimal furniture in its front windows to the clean lines of its display cabinets, items are artfully arranged to accent rather than overwhelm this small space. Owner Sarah Hammond loved to shop before she had a shop and her evangelism is evident in the sourcing. Homeware is overwhelmingly British - throws from Welsh weavers, furniture from a Nottingham-based company's 1960's back-catalogue – and surprisingly reasonable (£25 for a Mimi clasp purse, £8 an Orla Kiely mug, playful Ken Eardley ceramics minimally marked-up). A decade as a designer scavenger has given her practised hands, an ear for new names - she stocked Jen Rowland's bold graphics long before Liberties – and an eye for interiors with ceramics, candles, wallets and cards sitting low, and bags and bold graphic cushions residing high on reclaimed British Rail luggage racks. A unique boutique, elegant and chic. *TT*

MAP 19 Ref. 35

Cosi
85 Fortis Green Road
Muswell Hill N10 3HP
+44 (0)20 8883 2892
www.cosi-homewares.co.uk
Mon–Sat 10–5.30pm

Emporium Teas

Coffee shop doesn't do this justice. It is a destination point. A nostalgic hijack. A community cornerstone. Set up a year ago by two mums it is by definition local – everything from the art on the wall to the staff and regulars, to the tea on the trolley (from nearby W Martin). During the day it hums with the smell of fresh baking and bustling custom (it is hugely kid friendly). Tables are square and pretty, walls are clapperboard-clean and hung with the season's current art exhibition. At nights and weekends the overspill room transforms into a party venue-cum-craft workshop and sometime mythical storytelling haunt. Menus are pretension-free - porridge and golden syrup (£3.25), toast and Marmite (£1), but specials show a seasonal flair and an Afternoon Tea (a cake-stand of finger sandwiches, brownies and cakes with teas, £14 each, book in advance) is the stuff of lore and legend. *TT*

MAP 19 Ref. 37

Emporium Tea Rooms
4/5 Cheapside
Fortis Green
Muswell Hill N2 9HP
+44 (0)20 8883 3434
www.emporiumtearooms.co.uk
Mon–Sun 9–5pm

O Baby

There is a lot of superfluous baby 'stuff' out there. Happily, the ethos and space constraints at **O Baby** means they have whittled down your options to a few, choice, scrupulously sourced, ethical necessities (real nappies, potties, slings, washes, sleepbags, Sophie giraffes etc.) plus a beautiful clothing line and small but perfectly formed selection of traditional toys. Scandinavian in look and feel (stripped wooden shelves/floors, recessed lighting) O Baby is a resolutely customer-geared experience – a basket of toys on the floor, an unseen toilet out back, and 'Fancy a game of netball?' request on the cash till. Clothing lines - Green Baby, Minymo, Ej Sikke Lej, Littlechook, Piccalilly - are unusual and covetable, Fairtrade and 80 per cent organic. And toys (a DIY cardboard house) encourage imagination rather than passive button pushing. Expect heavy through-traffic from loyal, locals where this is, deservedly, a byword in trust and good taste. *TT*

MAP 19 Ref. 36

O Baby
126 Fortis Green Road
Muswell Hill N10 3DU
+44 (0)20 8444 8742
Mon–Sat 9.30–5.30pm

Sally Bourne Interiors

Sally Bourne caters to everything 'home' from the paint on your walls and curtain swag to tiling, blinds, the earthenware in your cupboard and candles on the sideboard. The ceiling-to-floor rolls of upholstery fabric detail the shop's 'working' nature with a central dias for fabric cutting and tile and paint stations. Bourne's hugely knowledgeable staff can navigate you through all their 12,000 shades of Farrow&Ball, Designers Guild, Sanderson's paints and a comprehensive consultancy service is available for more advanced interior aid. This is more than off the peg designer application - genuine creativity abounds. Ribbon spools are displayed in aluminium guttering, card stock is kept in wooden crates and wallpaper rolls hang from custom-made, Shaker-inspired coat pegs. The shop's signature style is evident everywhere from the visionary window displays to beautiful bundles of kindling (£5.95). I'm tempted. And I don't even own a fire. *TT*

MAP 19 Ref. 33

Sally Bourne Interiors
26 The Broadway
Muswell Hill N10 3RT
+44 (0)20 8444 3031
www.sallybourneinteriors.co.uk
Mon–Sat10–6pm
Sun 12–5pm

Second Nature feels thematic, like a museum. Although its contents can loosely be described as garden ephemera – flowers, planters, candles, container solutions - you navigate it like a visitor; reverential, respectful; here a family of sepia prints, a 'butterfly corner' (notebooks, desk calendars, specimens), there, a Wellington-fronted egg collector cabinet with replica eggs. There is a taxonomist's touch to everything – stuff collected, catalogued then lost again to the jumble of competing items from gardeners kneelers to first edition Penguin prints (£14). Everything is either beautiful, old or useful. Often all three. Orchids grow from vintage tea caddies. Brown paper Heritage Seeds (£2 each) sit in sifting trays. Up on a peg a Rectory folding chair makes a makeshift store for candles, bubble-bath, soaps. It smells of clove oil and the seasonal flowers Parker makes up in arrangements as bespoke and beautiful as the tiny space he so joyously curates. *TT*

MAP 19 Ref. 34
Second Nature
79 Fortis Green Road
Muswell Hill N10 3HP
+44 (0)20 8444 1717
Tue–Sat 9–6pm
Sun–Mon 11–4.30pm

Indish

Shakespeare may have counselled putting away childish things but **Indish** springs the toy chest to revive that essence of childhood – play, colour, invention – and make it a requisite for their resolutely grown up, designer stock. This small Crouch End institution has, for 15 years, been bringing colour to the burbs courtesy of Marimekko napkins, ISAK lovebird cups (£9.50) and MAGIS brooms in bold, primary hues. A shop of giftware, domestic designer-ware (Flos, Kartell, Pigeon lighting, an £80 Jacob Jenson smoke alarm anyone?) and visual punditry (the Bookrest Lamp and Thelermont Hupton's hang-loose coat-hook) its stock changes seasonally and is designed to tickle its punters and accommodate every pocket be that a Magis Deja-vu table by Naoto Fukasawa (£1,115) or a £2.50 Japanese panda paper balloon. *TT*

MAP 18 Ref. 26

Indish
16 Broadway Parade
Crouch End N8 9DE
+44 (0)20 8340 1188
www.indish.co.uk
Mon–Sat 10.30–5.30pm
Sun 12.30–4.30pm

Ever spent lazy afternoons rummaging through the French Brocante markets? Us neither. But lucky for us **Little Paris**' owners do, regularly, and recreate a fiction immeasurably more beautiful than actual fact. Owner Helene Allen wanted to make a space that embodied the spirit of her homeland and she succeeds. Accessories - leather handbags and silk scarves by young designers that she follows avidly and buys modestly (one, maybe two to keep her lines exclusive) – recall the street stalls of the Left Bank while the rest of the shop evokes a rambling, rural market. Pieces range from substantial-to-small – burnished industrial drawers (£950), a cow garden statue (£130) and vintage advertising posters (£10) for those of us without a chateau to refurbish. Weekends attract bargain-hungry Brits and French expatriates who congregate here informally – visibly relaxing amongst all that beauty. *TT*

MAP 18 Ref. 30
Little Paris
39 Park Road
Crouch End N8 8TE
+44 (0)20 8340 9008
www.littleparis.co.uk
Mon 11–6pm
Tue–Fri 10–6pm
Sat 10.30–6pm
Sun 11–5pm

-10%
*Discount**

Sable d'Or

Sable d'or Patisserie recalls the opening frames of Chocolat – the curved frontage, the marbled counter tops, the little confectionary creations in their paper casing cuffs. Inside it smells of fresh ground coffee and melted butter from the baking that happens here daily (chocolate gateaux, cheesecakes, butter croissants). Pretty waitresses ferry cleansing juices (at a very reasonable £2.50) and breakfast orders of crepes, brioches, open sandwiches between two well proportioned rooms and small tables that inspire intimate clinches and a low, respectful hubub. The atmosphere is continental, convivial, unhurried and, like it's sister shop in Muswell Hill, it shares a signature look of whitewashed walls, exposed brickwork, tiled floors and artwork by local talent. Cold drinks are top quality – Pukka, Chegworth Valley, James White – and the coffee is frothy and transporting. *TT*

MAP 18 Ref. 27

Sable d' Or
43 The Broadway
Crouch End N8 8DT
+44 (0)20 8341 7789
Mon–Sun 8–6pm

The Haberdashery

You know when you start selling name-brand jute bags that you have graduated from being a venue to a brand; a by-word for relaxation. **The Haberdashery** inspires a lifestyle loyalty from its clientèle. From the mismatched furniture and hot drinks in jam jars, to a scratchy vinyl soundtrack it leaves the polish and perfection to Starbucks and instead gives permission to unwind. Actors and creatives huddle in the high vaulted cafe (strung-bunting, fairy lights, pretty folding chairs) or the cobbled yard out back fuelled by home-baked pastries (polenta bread in terracotta pots) and Massimo's rocket-fuel (all the coffee is by Bristot - a small niche coffee maker from northern Italy). At night the cafe becomes an intimate venue for parties/weddings/ bazaars and exhibitions with a full liquor license (cocktails in vintage china cups) and wait-staff who recall Vincent Gallo in candy-striped aprons. The spirit of early New York, in N8. *TT*

MAP 18 Ref. 29

The Haberdashery
22 Middle Lane
Crouch End N8 8PL
+44 (0)20 8342 8098
www.the-haberdashery.com
Mon–Fri 8–6pm
Sat–Sun 9–6pm

The Workshop

Somehow, what with women's lib and working mothers, we managed to mislay an entire generation of teachers and with them the ability to make our own clothes/curtains/furniture/soap. **The Work Shop** seeks to practically re-parent; with groups and courses in mending and making running out of their Geppetto-style work room with a big table for cutting, bank of sewing machines and haberdashery drawers stuffed full of sandpaper, hairdryers and tools. Courses, craft parties and a regular Thursday night sew-cial (£6) congregate under the blackboard to the clinking of coffee cups and click-clacking of industry. Downstairs is the sofa and coffee area (magazines and books) while the shop-floor houses pretty rolls of fabric, reconditioned 'eco' sewing machines (all handcranks and spindles from £72) and a small but perfectly formed stock-line of wadding, wools, buttons and ribbons that whisper of quilts, as yet un-made. *TT*

MAP 18 Ref. 28
The Work Shop
10 Middle Lane
Crouch End N8 8PL
+44 (0)20 8340 3333
www.sallybourneinteriors.co.uk
Tue–Sat 10–6pm
except Thu 10–10pm

Casino

There's a thoroughly modern mashup going down at **Casino**, the mix including all you'd expect from an old-school retro store alongside brand new labels. If it's not vintage then it's got a vintage twist. Dresses from *Recycle & Reinvent* combine stretch jersey with recycled cotton prints or salvaged t-shirts to make a clothes rail worth a good perusal, as no two items seem the same. North London designers *emilyandfin* use end-of-line fabrics for their dresses and so get the thumbs-up for successful scavenging as they produce items in 'thriftful' limited editions. There are baseball jackets from LA, ski sweaters with snowflakes, tartan shirts and '80s jumpers. *Brat & Suzie* sweatshirts, designed to "go with everything" are adorned with cute animal illustrations. It's a gamble who you'll encounter in Casino. The stock is age-defying. Don't believe it? See the *nippazwithattitude* bibs and bodyvests. Strictly for the under-twos, Mutha-sucka. *GT*

MAP 20 Ref. 44

Casino
136 Stoke Newington
Church Street
Stoke Newington N16 0JU
+44 (0)20 7923 2225
www.casinovintage.com
Sun–Fri 11–6pm
Sat 10–6pm

Hub has two clothing outlets, each with its own distinctive character, within shouting distance of one another. To the north is the reassuringly old-fashioned men's shop. The appearance of a gentlemen's outfitters is consistent with the service: unobtrusive but available for those who require it. Clothes for the urbane but rugged man about town are well-made, of fine fabric and this lady writer could happily spend all day there, running her hands over the orderly piles of denim and woollens. The women's shop is equally welcoming and easy to navigate. Both have a mix of solid everyday staples – *Lee, Acne* and *Dr Denim* – punctuated by the eye-catching, such as *Something Else* for women and *Jacey Withers* jewellery for men. There's a British-made bias which includes Hub's own labels *Yarn* and *Beth Graham*. Producing as few as ten of any one item makes these pieces exclusively good value. *GT*

MAP 20 Ref. 40

Hub
49 Stoke Newington
Church Street
Stoke Newington N16 0AP
+44 (0)20 7254 4494
www.hubshop.co.uk
Mon–Sat 10.30–6.30pm
Sun 11–5pm

Mudfoot & Scruff

Ladies, men's and children's shoes, all under one roof, on one floor and well-displayed in a light and airy showroom. Almost unbelievable. But here it is. The spread of brands encompasses practical to quirky, and many are both. Predominantly European, many British and with an occasional highlight from the U.S., this selection shows a fascination for design that permeates the store. As with many independents, **Mudfoot & Scruff** is a family business that grew from the owners' own needs and what they felt to be lacking in their local marketplace. It's a tranquil, welcoming and comfortable space with a spare interior that makes for easy browsing, showing off the footwear to its best advantage. If your need for comfort, craftsmanship and good materials equals your passion for style, you'll appreciate the many obscure as well as familiar names including Dutch label Grotesque and new Brits on the block Rakish Heels and Esska. *GT*

MAP 20 Ref. 43

Mudfoot & Scruff
166 Stoke Newington
Church Street
Stoke Newington N16 0JL
+44 (0)20 7241 3009
Mon–Sat 11–6pm
Sun 11–5pm

Of Cabbages & Kings

Quietly out of the way, **Of Cabbages & Kings** is tucked around the corner from the well-trodden Church Street. Its appearance as gift shop belies its true identity of craft and art gallery. Fine art prints by local illustrators make up the core of its stock, mostly in limited editions. As is often the case with designers who aren't producing for a mass-market, the work is all the more appealing for being so individual and undiluted in style. Unusual jewellery and ceramics are likewise often produced locally and in small numbers, making them exclusive despite the competitive pricing. With so many designer-makers in the area, a monthly market in nearby Abney Hall has been set up to accommodate the overspill from the shop. See Of *Cabbages & Kings'* website for dates. For particular presents and distinctive objects for the home, it's well worth a deviation from the main drag. *GT*

MAP 20 Ref. 42
Of Cabbages & Kings
34b Kersley Road
Stoke Newington N16 0NH
+44 (0)20 7254 0060
www.ofcabbages.co.uk
Tue–Sat 11–6pm
Sun 1–5pm

Olive Loves Alfie

Olive loves Alfie isn't just clothes for kids. A visit for children's things is as likely to result in a new dress by *Marimekko* or all the christmas shopping in one fell swoop. Owner Ashlyn is not a fan of throw-away culture so everything is chosen with hand-me-down potential in mind. Many of the labels stocked use organic cotton – see *Monkey Genes* and the often entertaining *Mini-Rodini* – others are Fairtrade. The minefield of provenance has been picked through by Ashlyn and she can answer queries on these details. Beautifully illustrated books on wildlife and nature reflect a keen sense of aesthetics and make sense in a shop full of fun camping accessories. Nearly everything can be purchased via the comprehensive and inspiring website but a visit is a treat, if only to appreciate the variety of child-focused original artwork available to commission, great for those extra-special gifts. *GT*

MAP 20 Ref. 41

Olive Loves Alfie
84 Stoke Newington
Church Street
Stoke Newington N16 0AP
+44 (0)20 7241 4212
www.olivelovesalfie.co.uk
Mon–Fri 9.30–5.30pm
Sat 10–6pm
Sun 12–5pm

Pictures & Light

Many pictures. Fewer lights. Quite a lot of ceramics. Some glassware and a fair smattering of delicate jewellery. All very organised. Tidy. And neat. From among a stack of prints, one in particular calls for attention, its letters pressed in grainy woodblock type. Says William Morris "Have nothing in your home that you do not know to be useful, or believe to be beautiful". And there is the summation of things at **Pictures & Light**. If it's not one, it's the other. Specifically, lights are from the 1960s and '70s and cost up to £150. Pictures, or rather prints, are mostly Czech or Spanish language posters – vintage graphics, cherry-picked for their chalky colours and bold words. Most wonderful are the framed sheets culled from music scores, film journals and technical manuals of the last century. Never before has *Practical Wireless* seemed so beautiful. *GT*

MAP 20 Ref.39

Pictures & Light
41 Stoke Newington
Church Street
Stoke Newington N16 0NX
+44 (0)20 7923 7923
Thu–Sun 11–6pm

Rouge

Rouge offers a joyful splash of colour on an otherwise pallid English pavement. Owner Lei, a design graduate of Kingston University, is from Beijing and her buying ethos favours vivid hues and handicraft. She sources homewares, furniture and accessories from Japan, Vietnam and Thailand but predominantly rural China where she pursues the dwindling stock of reclaimed and reconditioned rustic furniture which dominates her range. As such she can advise customers on origins or suggest new pieces made from sustainably sourced wood. Aside from the painted wardrobes and chests is an array of delicate ceramics, hand-painted cards and ephemera, origami sets, automata and children's fabric bootees, toys and animals featuring appliqué and embroidery designs. The selection is noticeably different to anything on offer in Chinatown and has been chosen with the modern European home in mind, there being also a sister shop in central Brussels. *GT*

MAP 20 Ref. 38
Rouge
158 Stoke Newington
High Street
Stoke Newington N16 7JL
+44 (0)20 7275 0887
www.rouge-shop.co.uk
Mon–Sat 11–6.30pm
closed on Tue
Sun 12–5pm

The Tea Rooms

Yes, that name is plural. Not one, but two, exceedingly big rooms. Further tables in the garden only add to the relaxing space of these traditional **Tea Rooms**. Clientele clearly enjoy the old-fashioned set-up and the conversations that accompany the chink of china are always gentle. Pâtissière Isabelle Alfrey believes afternoon tea is a treat, and as such won't scrimp on quality or quantity. Her cake-stands heave with all manner of fruit, chocolate and nut permutations and the companion brew, chosen from a list of 20 or so teas featuring Darjeeling and Pu-erh, should refresh the most jaded palate. Meanwhile, a wandering eye can feast on the huge range of Poole pottery, collected by her mum, a published expert on the subject. Leaving without a memento isn't really an option. Those who resist the china, will most likely fall at the final hurdle of house jams, loose-leaf teas and crumbling fudge. *GT*

MAP 20 Ref. 45

The Tea Rooms
153–155 Stoke Newington Church Street
Stoke Newington N16 0UH
+44 (0)20 7923 1870
www.thetearooms.org
Tue–Fri 11–6pm
Sat–Sun 11–6.30pm

Push

"A bicycle shop that's a bit different" they say. We'd say they've taken the bicycle repair space from perfunctory to perfect. Push is a graphic designer's layout come alive. Every item is in its place, aligned to the grid. It even bears its own typeface. Such design conscious attention to fine detail is reflected throughout their selection of stock. The day-glo mainstream is relegated in preference for über-considered clothing brands such as *swrve* "urban cycling apparel" and helmets by *Yakkay* and *Bern*, all of whom value form as highly as functionality. Bikes on offer include the hand-crafted steel frames of British company *Mercian*, this being their chosen London outlet. With 3 mechanics always on duty, the priority at Push is immediate attention to service and they welcome enquiries regarding restoration of old bikes, a personal passion. *GT*

MAP 21 Ref. 47

Push
35c Newington Green
Newington Green N16 9PR
+44 (0)20 7249 1351
www.pushcycles.com
Mon–Fri 8–6pm
Sat 9–5.30pm

Three Potato Four

Opposite the climbing frames and swings of Newington Green is the indoor play space of **Three Potato Four**. This children's shop caters for all ages, in fact well into adulthood – who could fail to be happily regressed at the sound of a vintage Fisher Price record player? With a bias towards boys' toys (the owners have a son) and clothing in general, they also do big boys haircuts: the Sunday special is a father and child cut for £25. Kids can watch DVDs while dad sups on a cappuccino. A relationship with the café next door and a shared terrace makes for a cheerful and sociable environment. It's very relaxed and the seasonal Santa's Grotto is huge fun. While there's a great variety of clothing labels, footwear is a clear focus and they give a lot of space to family toiletries, stationery, books, artwork and baby gifts. *GT*

MAP 21 Ref. 46
Three Potato Four
44-45 Newington Green
Newington Green N16 9QH
+44 (0)20 7704 2228
www.threepotatofour.co.uk
Mon–Fri 10–5.30pm
Sat 9.30–7pm
Sun 11–6pm

Tina, We Salute You

The eponymous Tina, high priestess of Sixties sultriness, presides over all proceedings at this Dalston coffee-house that's definitely worth a slide off the track. From her gilt frame, with an eye towards the throbbing pavements of Kingsland High Street, she beckons. And they come. In defiance of the heretofore overlooked location, this is now a destination to beat towards. Sunny staff, cheerful chatter and coffee made with love. Rain or shine, **Tina, We Salute You** is a congenial corner. Fight for the marmite at the communal table. Rock up for rays at a pavement pew. Snuggle on the sofa. Perch by the glass. Goddamnit, grab a takeaway and sip it by the bike racks. Is there nothing wrong with this place? Did I mention the cakes? Lush. Homemade! And getting ever more elaborate. But hurry, because that menu changes with the wind. And the art… come see for yourself. *GT*

MAP 21 Ref. 48

Tina, We Salute You
47 King Henry's Walk
Dalston N1 4NH
+44 (0)20 3119 0047
www.tinawesaluteyou.com
Tue–Fri 8–7pm
Sat 9–7pm
Sun 10–7pm

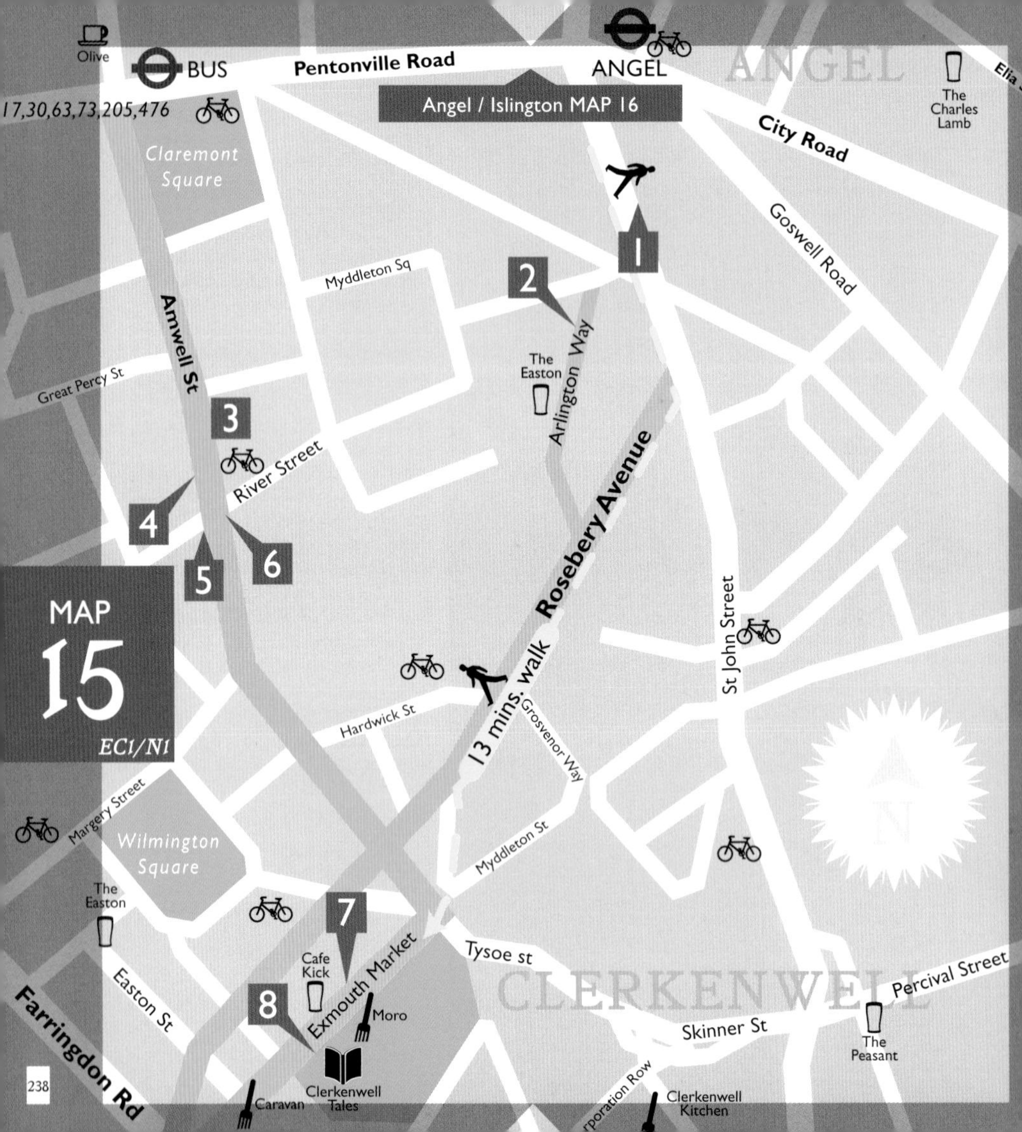
Olive
BUS
17,30,63,73,205,476
Pentonville Road
ANGEL
Angel / Islington MAP 16
ANGEL
The Charles Lamb
Elia St
City Road
Claremont Square
Goswell Road
Myddleton Sq
1
2
The Easton
Arlington Way
Great Percy St
Amwell St
3
River Street
Rosebery Avenue
4
5
6
MAP
15
EC1/N1
St John Street
13 mins. walk
Hardwick St
Grosvenor Way
Margery Street
Wilmington Square
Myddleton St
The Easton
7
Tysoe st
Cafe Kick
8
Exmouth Market
Moro
Easton St
Farringdon Rd
CLERKENWELL
Percival Street
Skinner St
The Peasant
Clerkenwell Tales
Caravan
Clerkenwell Kitchen

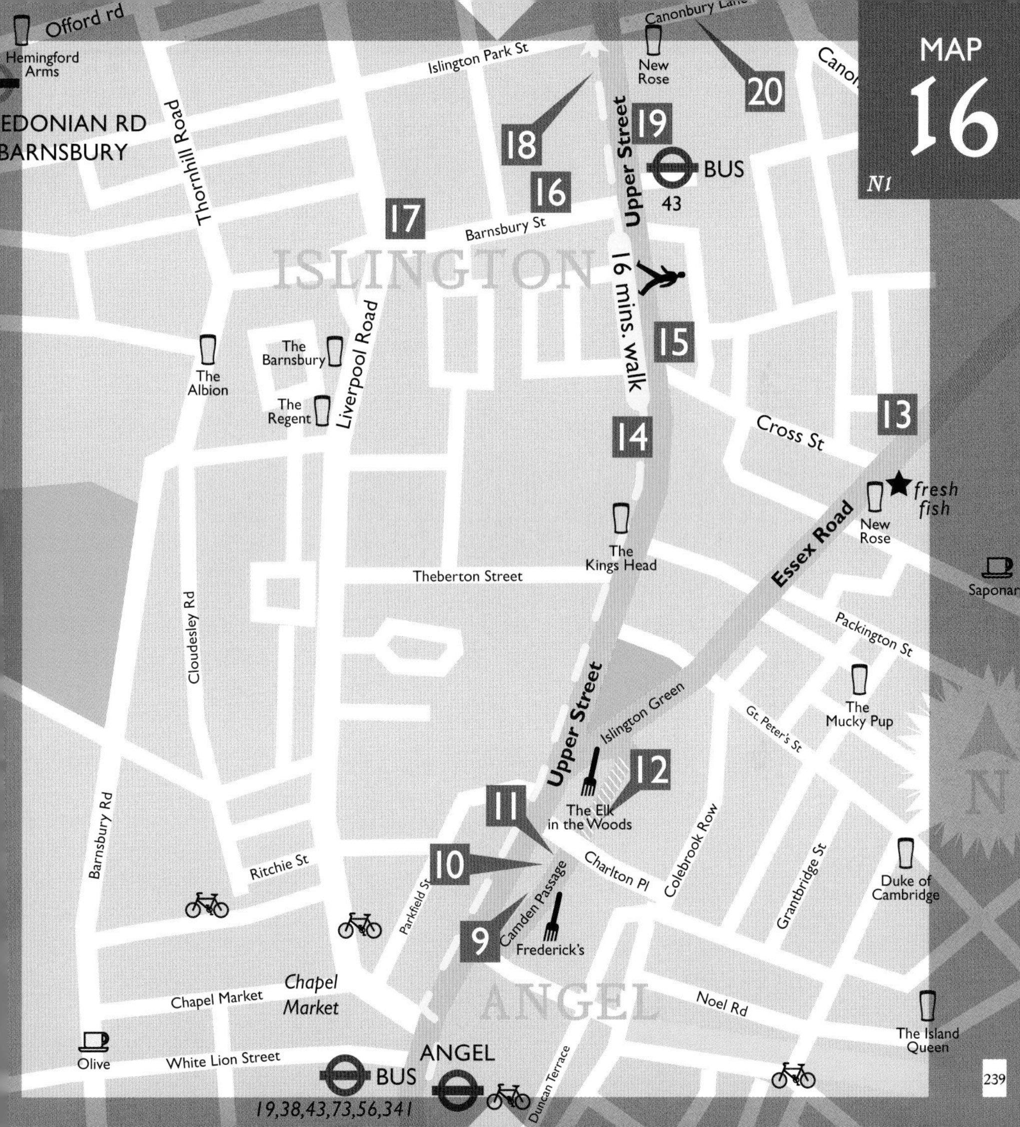
MAP
16
N1
Offord rd
Hemingford Arms
CALEDONIAN RD
BARNSBURY
Canonbury Lane
Canon
Islington Park St
New Rose
20
18
19
16
17
BUS
43
Thornhill Road
Upper Street
Barnsbury St
ISLINGTON
16 mins. walk
15
The Albion
The Barnsbury
The Regent
Liverpool Road
13
14
Cross St
fresh fish
New Rose
The Kings Head
Essex Road
Theberton Street
Saponara
Cloudesley Rd
Packington St
The Mucky Pup
Upper Street
Islington Green
Gt. Peter's St
12
Barnsbury Rd
11
The Elk in the Woods
Colebrook Row
10
Charlton Pl
Ritchie St
Parkfield St
Camden Passage
Grantbridge St
Duke of Cambridge
9
Frederick's
Chapel Market
Chapel Market
ANGEL
Noel Rd
The Island Queen
Olive
White Lion Street
ANGEL
BUS
19,38,43,73,56,341
Duncan Terrace

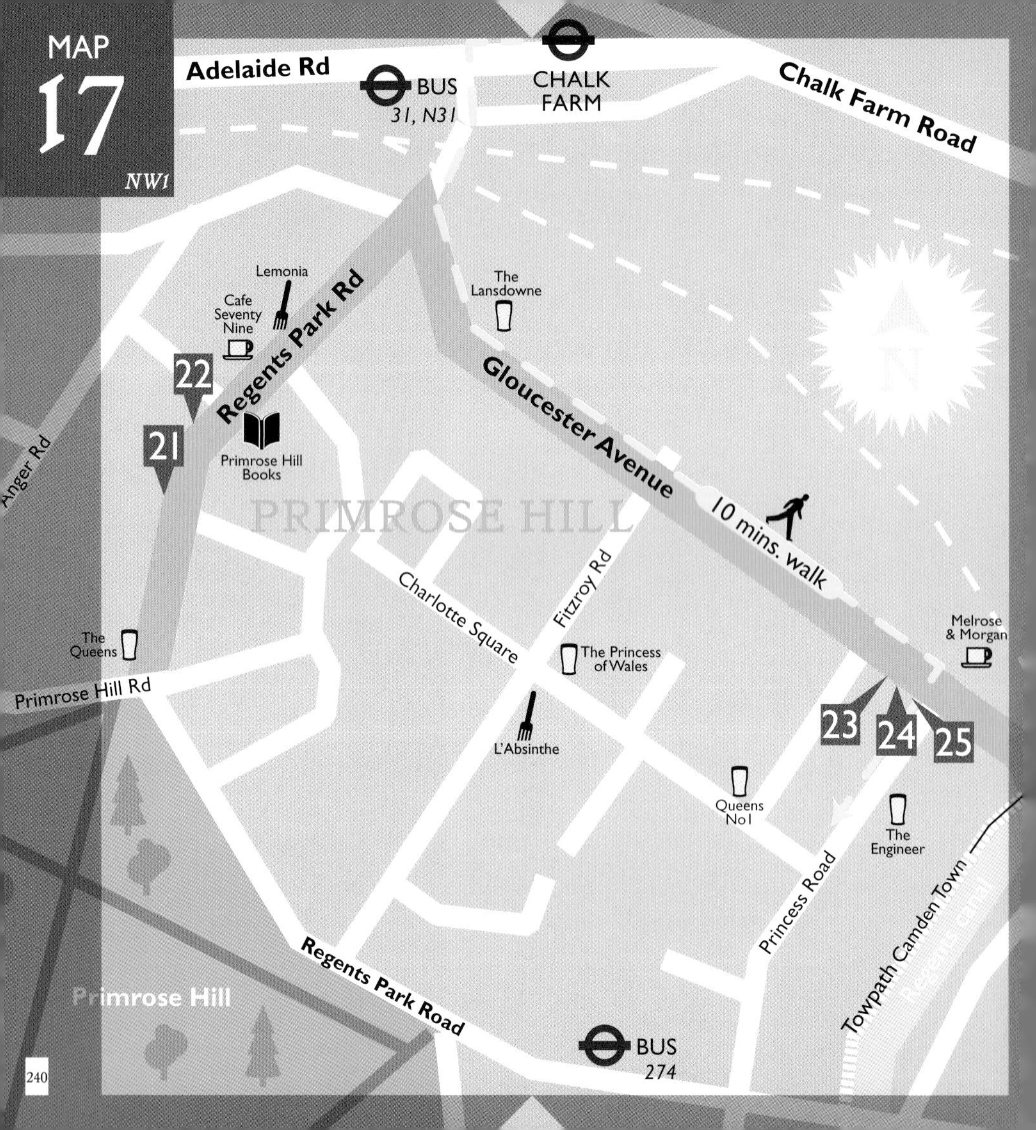

MAP

17

NW1

Adelaide Rd

BUS
31, N31

CHALK FARM

Chalk Farm Road

Lemonia

Cafe Seventy Nine

Regents Park Rd

The Lansdowne

Gloucester Avenue

22

21

Primrose Hill Books

Anger Rd

PRIMROSE HILL

10 mins. walk

Charlotte Square

Fitzroy Rd

The Queens

The Princess of Wales

Melrose & Morgan

Primrose Hill Rd

L'Absinthe

23

24

25

Queens No1

The Engineer

Princess Road

Towpath Camden Town

Regents canal

Regents Park Road

Primrose Hill

BUS
274

MAP 18

N8

Alexandra Park

Priory Road

Priory Park

CROUCH END

Muswell Hill MAP 19

29 mins. walk

Park Road

Lynton Rd

Middle Lane

Tottenham Lane

28

29

Coffee Cake

Elder Ave

Broadway Parade

Banner's

30

26

27

Middle Lane

BUS

W1,W5,41,91

King's Head

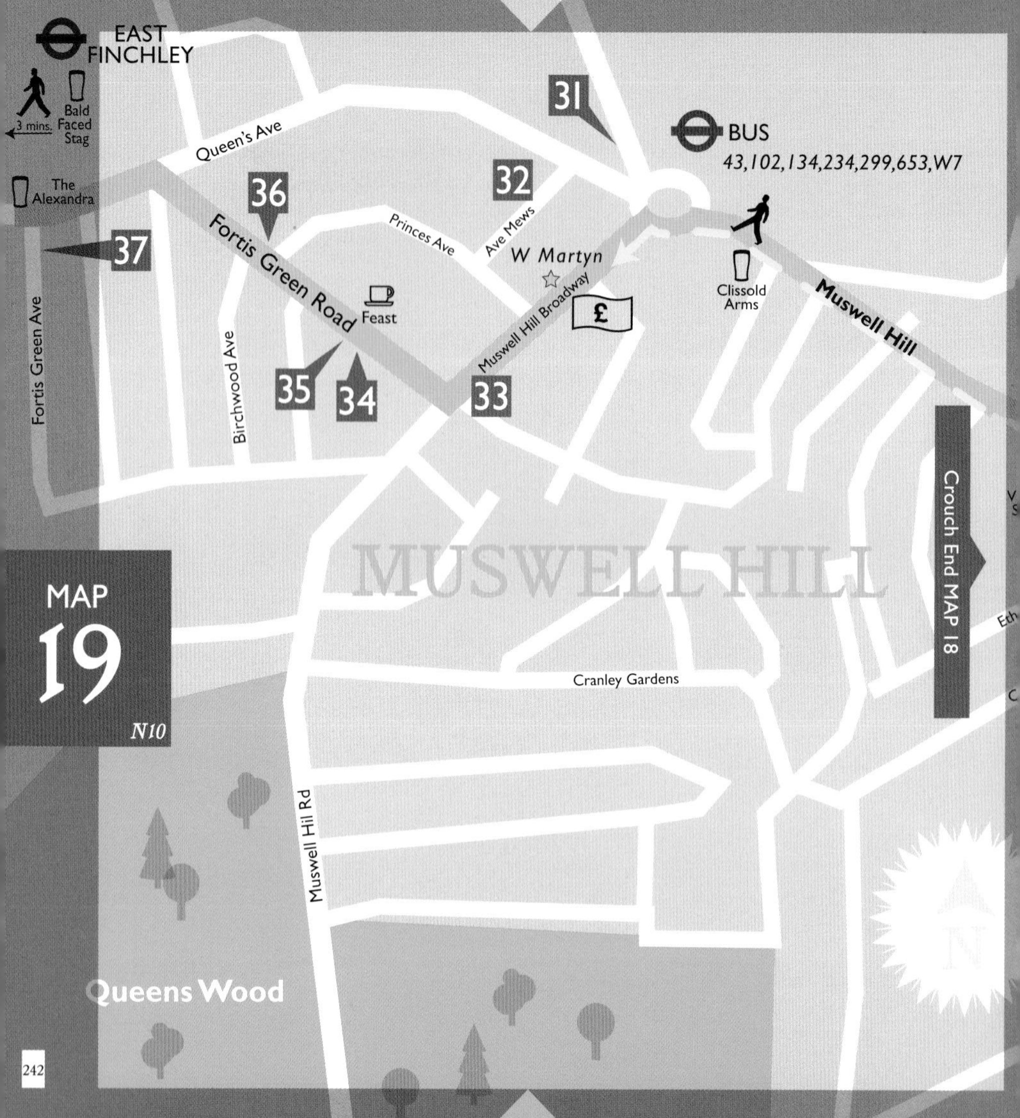
EAST FINCHLEY
3 mins.
Bald Faced Stag
The Alexandra
Queen's Ave
31
36
32
37
BUS
43,102,134,234,299,653,W7
Princes Ave
Ave Mews
W Martyn
Fortis Green Road
Muswell Hill Broadway
Feast
£
Clissold Arms
Muswell Hill
Fortis Green Ave
Birchwood Ave
35
34
33
Crouch End MAP 18
MUSWELL HILL
MAP
19
N10
Cranley Gardens
Muswell Hil Rd
Queens Wood

MAP
20
N16
STOKE
NEWINGTON
Jolly
Butcher
Abney Park
Cemetery
Lordship Rd
The
Lion
Daniel
Defoe
41
43
Church St
40
39
Lemon
Monkey
44
Stoke Newington
Homa
Rasa
Lancell St
Farmers
Market
(Saturdays)
£
Clissold Park
Cakes
45
42
Coach &
Horses
Defoe Rd
Kersley Rd
Stoke Newington
Bookshop
Clissold Park
The
Spence
Woodlea Rd
Church St.
Bookshop
38
fresh
fish
The
Prince
Church St
STOKE
NEWINGTON
fish&
chips
Clissold Rd
Stoke Newington High St
BUS
3,393,476
The
Londesborough
25 mins. walk
Evering Rd
Dalston MAP 21
The

MAP
21
E8/N16
Stoke Newington MAP 20
The Shakespeare
Allen Rd
Albion Road
Shakespeare walk
Stoke Ne
Lanes
Trattoria Sapori
Ruby Blue
47
46
Moustache bar
Arcola Theatre
Barrets Grove
Marquis of Lansdowne
Mangal Oca Turkish g
BUS
236
DALSTON
Bardens Boudoir
Pyrland Road
Newington Green
Boleyn Road
Somine Restaurant
Mildmay Road
Dalston Superstore
BU
67,76,149,24
Rio Cinema
Queen Margarets Grove
48
Grosvenor Ave
Newington Green Road
Alibi
Vortex Jazz Bar
Ridley Market
Ridley R
King Henry's Walk
The Alma
DALSTON KINGSLAND
Kingsland High St
CANONBURY
Cafe Oto
£
Balls Pond Rd
The Wellington
BUS
30,38,56,277
Dalst
DALSTON JUNCTION
Scolt Head
Visions Video Bar

W Martyn 135 Muswell Hill, Broadway N10 / www.wmartyn.co.uk

London Glassblowing Workshop Bermondsey (Page 266)

SE10 Greenwich
SE10/SE14 Deptford
SE22 East Dulwich
SE1 Waterloo
SE1 Bermondsey
SE1 Borough
SW4 Clapham

Layne, artisan glassblower at the **London Glassblowing Workshop** working on his latest piece. Handcrafts like this have seen a great increase throughout London.

The Cheeseboard

Royal Hill boasts a thread of high-quality food shops, which sell produce that is a million miles away from that found on the shelves of Tesco. The **Cheeseboard** sits a few doors along from Drings Butcher – both owned by Mike Jones, who has experience and passion for good quality food produce. The shop – open since 1985 – offers over 100 varieties of English and Continental cheeses and the knowledgeable staff are on-hand to offer their best cheesy advice. Freshly baked artisan bread is displayed above the cheese counters and the country-style baskets below are filled with traditional oatcakes and savoury biscuits. There's a good selection of chutneys, pickles and olives available and you can buy wine here too as well as a hand picked selection of pale ales and beers. *RL*

MAP 22 Ref. 5
The Cheeseboard
26 Royal Hill
Greenwich SE10 8RT
+44 (0)20 8305 0401
www.cheese-board.co.uk
Mon–Wed 9–5pm
Thu 9–1pm Fri 9–5.30pm
Sat 8.30–4.30pm

Cherry Picked is a unique designer boutique in Greenwich Market is very special indeed, Phyllis Taylor bought the shop over 5 years ago and has used her cultural background to bring a little slice of Ghana to London. Using fair-trade fabrics sourced from her parents' home town in Ghana, Phyllis has designed a capsule collection of women and children's clothing using classic 50s and 60s shapes. The 'Sika' label is based on simplicity and flattering feminine shapes and the clothing range is reasonably priced given its designer reputation. The Sika designs – which change seasonally – have been featured in Grazia, Vogue, East Living, You and the Daily Mirror – to name but a few. The combination of ethnic fabrics, retro shapes, made-to-measure designs (on request) and staff who truly care about the label, create an impressive, independent boutique worthy of a visit. *RL*

MAP 22 Ref. 1
Cherry Picked
5a Greenwich Market
Greenwich SE10 9HZ
+44 (0)20 8858 8158
www.sikadesigns.co.uk
Mon–Fri 12–6pm
Sat–Sun 12–6pm

Drings Butchers

Drings has a 45-year history and over the past four years Mike Jones has successfully managed to maintain its excellent reputation. If you only shop in supermarkets and think you've tasted 'proper' meat before, think again – the sausages here are all made on the premise and contain a minimum of 97% free-range pork. All of the meat is free-range and the pork and poultry is sourced from a reputable farm in Suffolk. Emphasis is on well-reared, good quality meat. You can expect a personal touch at Drings too – staff know their regular customers by name and you can even call in advance to pre-order cuts of meat if you have a specific dish in mind. *RL*

MAP 22 Ref. 4
Drings
22 Royal Hill
Greenwich SE10 8RT
+44 (0)20 8858 4032
www.drings.co.uk
Mon–Wed 9–5pm
Thu 9–1pm Fri 9–5.30pm
Sat 8.30–4.30pm

The Fishmonger

The Fishmonger is quietly tucked away in a village-style area away from the main tourist throng.

Not your usual fishmonger, this little fish shop offers a full selection of fresh, cooked and frozen fish, seafood, dressed crabs and tinned fish as well as gourmet accompaniments such as sauces, spices, sea salt, oils, vinegars, and fresh samphire. The fish is freshly sourced from a family-run business based on the Cornish coastline as well as Billingsgate Market. Sustainability is firmly in mind too – you certainly won't find bluefin tuna in this fishmonger. The fish is cut to order and staff can advise which are the best cuts available for sushi, should you like to try your hand at Japanese cuisine. *RL*

MAP 22 Ref. 6
The Fishmonger
Circus Street / rear of
26 Royal Hill
Greenwich SE10 8RT
+44 (0)7880 541485
www.thefishmongerltd.com
Tue–Fri 8.30–5pm
Sat 7.30–4.30pm

Pickwick Papers & Fabrics

This is the type of shop that will make you want to instantly redecorate your house and be creative. With an inspiring collection of unique wallpaper designs, fabrics, bedding, blinds, curtains, carpets and paint – you'll be stocking up your basket faster than you can say 'changing rooms'! Renowned as one of London's finest interior design shops, **Pickwick Papers & Fabrics** have been in business since 1985 and even offer an interior design service for those needing professional advice. Whatever your need, big or small, staff at Pickwick are happy to help. *RL*

MAP 22 Ref. 2
Pickwick Papers & Fabrics
6 Nelson Road
Greenwich SE10 9JB
+44 (0)20 8858 1205
www.pickwickpapers.co.uk
Tue–Sat 9.30–5pm
Sun 11–3pm

Royal Teas

Royal Teas is a rare gem in London: this cosy little café is the type of place where everyone knows your name if you're a regular – cheers! Of course you can remain incognito should that be your wish. The independent café boasts a predominately vegetarian menu that changes every other day. You can expect a tasty choice for breakfast, soups, salads, sandwiches, freshly-ground coffee and loose leaf and herbal teas. There's a reasonably-priced cream tea on the menu, as well as a dangerously tempting selection of cakes that are freshly made on the premise. As for the décor – brightly coloured exposed brick walls displaying local artwork, wooden floors and cosy little tables create a nice warm arty atmosphere. You can sit outside too, if the sun decides to shine. *RL*

MAP 22 Ref. 7

Royal Teas
76 Royal Hill
Greenwich SE10 8RT
+44 (0)20 8691 7240
www.royalteascafe.co.uk
Mon–Fri 9.30–5.30pm
Sun 10–6pm
Sun 10.30–6pm

Stitches & Daughters

Just a hop skip and a jump from Greenwich station, **Stitches & Daughters** provides a veritable treasure trove of homeware goods, gifts and classic designer clothing with a contemporary edge – just follow your nose. The shop houses a range of scented candles made by various companies, some relaxing, some rejuvenating and all impossible to put down without one last sniff. There's also a fabulous range of children's toys and irresistibly cute leather booties for babies as well as handmade cushions, carved wooden doorstoppers, unique gift wrap and pretty ribbons. This village-style shop is girly heaven, with its heady scents, pretty products and friendly staff. *RL*

MAP 22 Ref. 3

Stitches & Daughters
3 Greenwich South Street
Greenwich SE10 8NW
+44 (0)20 8305 1396
www.stitchesanddaughters.co.uk
Mon–Fri 10–5.30pm
Sat 10–5pm

Greenwich SE10 (Page 27 Map 22)
ROYAL HILL
ROYAL PLACE
17

Cod Father's/The Egg Shop

Cod Father's and **The Egg Shop** run by Bob and Dave 'Fish' has been a fixture on Deptford High Street since most can remember. Selling fresh fish out of one shop, eggs and apple juice supplied from his farm in Kent, out of the other. Deptford High streets is still one of the most 'original' and characterful high streets in London, full of 'hustle and bustle'. The Market, on Wednesdays and Saturdays is definitely a place for bargains – including fruit and veg, clothes and household items, be it with lessening variety as the market has seen some decline. Unfortunately the High street too, has developed the same blight as many other parts of London with too many betting shops and pound shops as well as the pubs closing.

MAP 21

The Egg Shop
49 Deptford High Street
London SE8 4AD
Tues–Sat 6am–4pm

Fairies & Floozies

Fairies and Floozies – one could be forgiven for thinking that this might be East Dulwich's first 'adult' shop. On the contrary, this is a chic little boutique tucked away down a quiet road next to the station, which sells an eclectic range of affordable designer clothing – with not a nipple tassel in sight. Leather belts, handmade jewellery, handbags and clothing from labels such as Religion, Max C, Yuki and T Style are displayed throughout the boudoir-style interior. Clothing and accessories are sourced by the owner who has 14 years' of solid fashion experience and the collection changes seasonally – giving us the perfect excuse to pop in on a regular basis. Also in tune with the local community, the shop arranges various events including 'styling nights' – you can't get more niche than that in East Dulwich. *RL*

MAP 23 Ref. 8

Fairies & Floozies
16 Melbourne Grove
East Dulwich SE22 8QZ
+44 (0)20 8299 3939
www.fairiesandfloozies.com
Mon–Fri 12–7pm
Sat 10–6.30pm
Sun 12.30–4.30pm

Franklins Farm Shop

Encapsulating the feel of a traditional village food store, **Franklin's Farm Shop** welcomes its visitors with rustic wicker baskets filled with colourful fruit and vegetables under a dark green awning. Inside, the authentic feel continues with sturdy wooden shelves, baskets and boxes full of tempting seasonal produce and gourmet ingredients for a complete and ethical meal. Husband and wife team Tim and Felicity joined up with Rodney Franklin and used their collective experience of the food industry to open Franklin's in 1999. They stock freshly baked bread, English cheeses, and some of the prettiest artisan cakes you'll ever see – all produce is locally sourced from within the UK. There's also a multi-award winning restaurant, which is renowned for providing a good quality simple menu. The lunches here have a great reputation. This shop redefines what good food should be: locally sourced and very high-quality. Supermarkets beware. *RL*

MAP 23 Ref. 11

Franklin's Farm Shop
155 Lordship Lane
East Dulwich SE22 8HX
+44 (0)20 8693 3992
www.franklinsrestaurant.com
Mon–Sun 9–5.30pm

Mrs Robinson

In the heart of East Dulwich a colourful cave of gifts, vintage Danish furniture, clothing, kitchen- and homeware awaits. The ceiling is adorned with colour-pop silk shades that can be made to order depending on your colour preference and the shelves are positively brimming with contemporary products that would make a quirky and modern addition to any home. The furniture section features an eclectic range of vintage leather sofas, coffee tables and retro lamps and towards the back of the shop there's also an extensive collection of decorative mirrors. In the back of the shop there is a menswear boutique selling a range of casual designer clothing and labels such as Calvin Klein. It doesn't end there – across the road **Mrs Robinson** also has a dedicated boutique for ladies selling classic designs for smart women who like their clothing a little edgy. *RL*

MAP 23 Ref. 10

Mrs Robinson
153 Lordship Lane
East Dulwich SE22 8HX
+44 (0)20 8613 1970
www.mrsrobinsons.co.uk
Mon–Sat 10–5.30pm
Sun 12–5pm

Reminiscent of an old apothecary, a visit to **Roullier White** is an all together pleasant experience. Visualise walls lined with vintage wooden cabinets filled with products that are both attractive and functional. The fresh floral notes from exclusive scented candles waft through the shop whilst the informative staff are on-hand to provide friendly advice – they can even tell you which perfume is the perfect choice for you. This lifestyle boutique is a unique and refreshing addition to south London, it opened five years ago and has since attracted an abundance of press coverage. They sell an eclectic range of goods ranging from kitchenware, exclusive perfumes, men's toiletries, bathroom products, jewellery and garden products. The owner's great grandma was the inspiration behind the Mrs White's range: products inspired by her natural recipes, remedies, notions and potions. Beautifully packaged and environmentally friendly it's difficult not to buy the entire range. *RL*

MAP 23 Ref. 9
Roullier White
125 Lordship Lane
East Dulwich SE22 8HU
+44 (0)20 8693 5150
www.roullierwhite.com
Mon–Sat 10–6pm
Sun 11–5pm

The Good Companion 27–29 Norwood Road, Herne Hill SE24 / www.thegoodcompanion.co.uk

With a tagline "All beautiful things made with love" this community embracing shop is about just that. All the products you will find here come from either locals or friends of the owner making '**Bermondsey Fayre**' a very apt name. Everything is ethically sourced, fair trade and handmade from paintings to clothes to chutney, giving the shop an arts and crafts feel. Regular workshops teaching an assortment of fun classes including making fancy knickers, sock monkeys, floral brooches and even your own beauty products keeps the theme of the shop eclectic and fun creating a real community spirit, "We think that rather than just being a shop it's a good opportunity to offer more than that". A great place to buy something both pleasing and handy is summed up in a photograph from a local photographer stating "Have nothing in your home that you do not know to be useful, or believe to be beautiful". *PB*

MAP 24 Ref. 17
Bermondsey Fayre
212 Bermondsey Street
Bermondsey SE1 3TQ
+44 (0)20 7403 2133
www.bermondseyfayre.co.uk
Wed–Sat 11.30–7pm

Named after the French word for 'wine cellar', **Cave** sells the quality things in life and is ideal for a little something to bring to a dinner party. They offer expert advice, proudly declaring, "We love to help people choose". A gap in the local market for designer fresh cut flowers, specially chosen wines and exquisite artisan chocolates ethically sourced presented itself and thus Cave was born. With a homely pared down English environment the shop smells delicious with flowers and autumn leaves.

All the wine is produced on a small scale and is bio-dynamic and organic and the shop packaging is 100% recycled and untreated, being good for the planet as well as stylish. Their products are very well thought out and edited so that every purchasing decision is a good one, "we know the market well round here, we have an aesthetic response to our community". *PB*

MAP 24 Ref. 16

Cave
210 Bermondsey Street
Bermondsey SE1 3TQ
+44 (0)20 0011 4701
www.cavelondon.com
Mon–Sat 10–8pm

Cockfighter of Bermondsey

A curious mix of council estates, high-end residential properties and converted warehouses, Bermondsey is the ideal spot for an edgy shop like the **Cockfighter of Bermondsey**. This playful and flirty boutique stocks a fashionable range of eye-catching men and woman's clothing from humorously camp skull and cross bone printed Y-fronts and frilly knickers to a selection of fifties-style bowling shirts and dresses. Branded under the Cockfighter and Cock & Magpie labels you'll find hats, belts, bags and jewellery alongside a range of branded and logo-ed T-shirts (with slogans such as 'honk if you had it last night'), denim and casual wear emblazoned with the distinctive Cockfighter logo. With a tight London theme including handmade cards which celebrate London scenes the clothes are named after London spots Shoreditch, Hackney and, of course, Bermondsey. *PB*

MAP 24 Ref. 15

Cockfighter of Bermondsey
96 Bermondsey Street
Bermondsey SE1 3UB
+44 (0)20 7357 6482
www.cockandmadpie.com
Tue by appointment
Wed & Sat 10–6pm
Thu–Fri 11–7pm
Sun 11–5pm

London Galssblowing Workshop could easily be mistaken as just an upmarket showroom displaying glassware is in fact one of the most innovative galleries around. With a gallery space upfront the back is a fully functioning workshop where visitors can bring a cup of coffee, pull up a chair and watch the process in action. Trained artisans in various stages of the procedure create stunning pieces in front of your eyes. An informal environment that bridges the gap between artist and viewer where they are happy to answer any questions you may have. Regular glassblowing classes are held where you can learn the process first hand along with evening events and exhibitions. Raging furnaces known as 'reheating chambers' or to the experts, 'Glory Holes' keep the room toasty warm so it's easy to get comfortable and while a way an afternoon watching molten glass transform into the exquisite pieces they have on display. *PB*

MAP 24 Ref. 14

London Glassblowing Workshop
62–66 Bermondsey Street
Bermondsey SE1 3UD
+44 (0)20 7403 2800
www.londonglassblowing.co.uk
Mon–Sat 10–5pm

Who said that moving had to be a pain? **The Rocketvan Boxshop** provides a full removal and delivery service and even makes buying boxes and packaging material that little bit more fun. A bit like being in a giant cardboard box, the interior of the shop is comprised of cardboard, varnished MDF and pegboard, traditionally used in old hardware stores. They have a straightforward system of choosing boxes that range in dimensions and material, either plastic or cardboard and in every size from extra-small to extra-large and everything you might need from room contents labels to bubble wrap, brown tape and string. They even have some cleverly picked out things like cardboard birdhouses, welcome mats, tea-lights and decorative wall prints to furnish a room, making it a little bit more homely. A quirky approach to branding, you wouldn't find space invaders on the wall of your local DHL would you? *PB*

MAP 24 Ref. 13
The Rocketvan Boxshop
229–231 Union Street
Borough SE1 3TQ
+44 (0)20 7401 3928
www.rocketvan.co.uk
Mon–Sat 8–6pm

It's not hard to fathom that in these fashionable times knitting will be right up there with fixed wheel bikes and warehouse raves as the latest thing considered the height of cool. Established by Craig who started knitting when he was seven, his first projects being clothes for his action men and Gerard who was confined to his couch with a back problem and needed something to do other than eat cake and watch telly, **I Knit** evolved from a community group with a shared love of knitting over a pint of beer. Offering weekly classes for beginners and fun social get-togethers with champagne (they have a liquor licence) and croissants for those with more experience to swap tips. With the largest selection of knitting books and magazines in London and shelves packed with different varieties of wool, I Knit stock everything on the list for the beginner to the advanced. *PB*

MAP 24 Ref. 12
I Knit
106 Lower Marsh
Waterloo SE1 7AB
+44 (0)20 7261 1338
www.iknit.org.uk
Mon 11–6pm
Tue–Thu 11–9pm
Fri–Sat 11–6pm

Birksen

Birksen is not just a flower shop; it is more of a lifestyle statement. As Birksen's philosophy says, "flowers make us happy". Here you won't just find the most beautiful and fresh tulips, peonies, dahlias or roses but also every single accessory that will frame your preferred arrangement in the best way as well as seeds, gardening equipment and an array of bits and pieces that will help you create a mini paradise on earth, even that special setting that you are after. Birksen also specialises in providing all flower arrangements for any kind of event: from weddings, to parties and corporate events, even magazine shoots. Staff are very friendly and will help you put together a nice bouquet if you want to win over that grumpy neighbour or impress the girl of your dreams; you don't even have to release your inner charmer. Birksen's flowers will do the work. *DG*

MAP 25 Ref. 19
Birksen
40 Old Town
Clapham SW4 0LB
+44 (0)20 7622 6466
www.birksen.co.uk
Mon–Fri 8.30–5.30pm
Sat 10–5pm
Sun 10.30–4pm

JZD is one of those boutiques that even if you don't intend on buying anything, you are sure not to leave empty-handed. Situated in Clapham's quaint old Town, it combines cool fashion and a bit of history. And who doesn't find that a bit tempting? Occupying a three-storey townhouse, which also happens to be Clapham's oldest building, JZD is filled with some of the coolest womenswear brands, like danish 'By Malene Birger', spanish 'Hoss Intropia', Trevor Bolongaro, affordable jewellery as well as cool menswear names, like Superdry and Gio Goi, makers of quirky t-shirts, or in other words 'cool things to go in your wardrobe and stay there for years'. It may be just over ten years old, but it has still got the buzz, as owners Raj Wilkinson and his wife Sam, a former Selfridges buyer, still scout the world for the coolest and funkiest offerings. One thing is for sure: you will come again, and again, and again. *DG*

MAP 25 Ref.20

JZD
45 Old Town
Clapham SW4 0JL
www.jzdstyle.co.uk
+44 (0)20 7720 8050
Mon–Wed 10–6pm
Thu–Fri 10–7pm
Sat 10-6:30pm
Sun 12-6pm

Les Sardines

Italian Leopoldina Haynes used to work at one of London's famous auction houses as a watches specialist, until she decided to give it all up to pursue her passion for interiors. Just a year old, **Les Sardines** specialises in French and Swedish antiques (for example, an 18th c French armoire or a 19th c chest of drawers) which Leopoldina searches out around the world using her keen eye, but also those small bits and pieces that make a difference; from vintage mugs and jugs, lavender pouches and linen cushion covers to Italian soaps, even cute, little notebooks. The best thing about the shop: its affordability factor (prices start at £5) and friendly vibe. As she says, 'Antiques can be off-putting but I wanted to create a place where anybody can buy anything, a place that makes you want to go away with something'. *DG*

MAP 25 Ref. 22

Les Sardines
63 Abbeville Road
Clapham SW4 9JW
+44 (0)20 8675 3900
www.lessardines.co.uk
Tue–Sat 10–6pm
Sun 12–4pm

M. Moen & Sons

A 39-year-old family business, now owned and run by Garry Moen, son of founder Maurice, **M. Moen & Sons** is one of Clapham's, if not London's, great butchers and delicatessen shops. For a start, the interior will blow you away: restored to its former Victorian glory with the help of a National Lottery grant, this place is filled with every kind of meat imaginable and of the highest quality: free-range or organic beef, own-made sausages, venison, poultry and game. And not just that, the shop also has a special section on cheeses and cold cuts, like Parma and Serrano ham as well as an amazing deli counter, where you can find pickles, mustards, chutneys and jams. Did we mention the weekly confit, pate and cassoulet deliveries from France? Or even the daily fruit and mushroom offerings from local independent farmers? M. Moen& Sons is not just a gourmet shop, but rather a precious address in your notebook if good quality nutrition is high on your agenda. *DG*

MAP 25 Ref. 21

M. Moen & Sons
24 The Pavement
Clapham SW4 0JA
+44 (0)20 7622 1624
www.moen.co.uk
Mon–Fri 8.30–6.30pm
Sat 8.30-5pm

Places & Spaces

Let's say you are after an Achille Castiglioni Arco 1962 lamp, or an Alvar Aalto vase, even a Verner Panton Tivoli dining chair. Well, Places and Spaces is definitely your place. A must shop for hardcore design aficionados, this shop plays host to a pretty fine collection of some of the most iconic pieces of 20th century design (anything from furniture to accessories and lighting). But its forte is not just cult design classics: **Places and Spaces** also sources and stocks modern favourites such as pieces by Droog or Ronan and Erwan Bouroullec to name just a few, positioning itself as the ultimate space for exploring design. Its trusted team will also provide help, should you decide to put all these old and modern classics under one roof and even create a unique look for your office or apartment. Should you want to delve more into the world of design, check out the frequent activities it organises, especially, the interesting design exhibitions it curates all around London. *DG*

MAP 25 Ref. 18

Places and Spaces
30 Old Town
Clapham SW4 OLB
+44 (0)20 7498 0998
www.placesandspaces.com
Tue–Sat 10–5.45pm
Sun 12 – 4pm

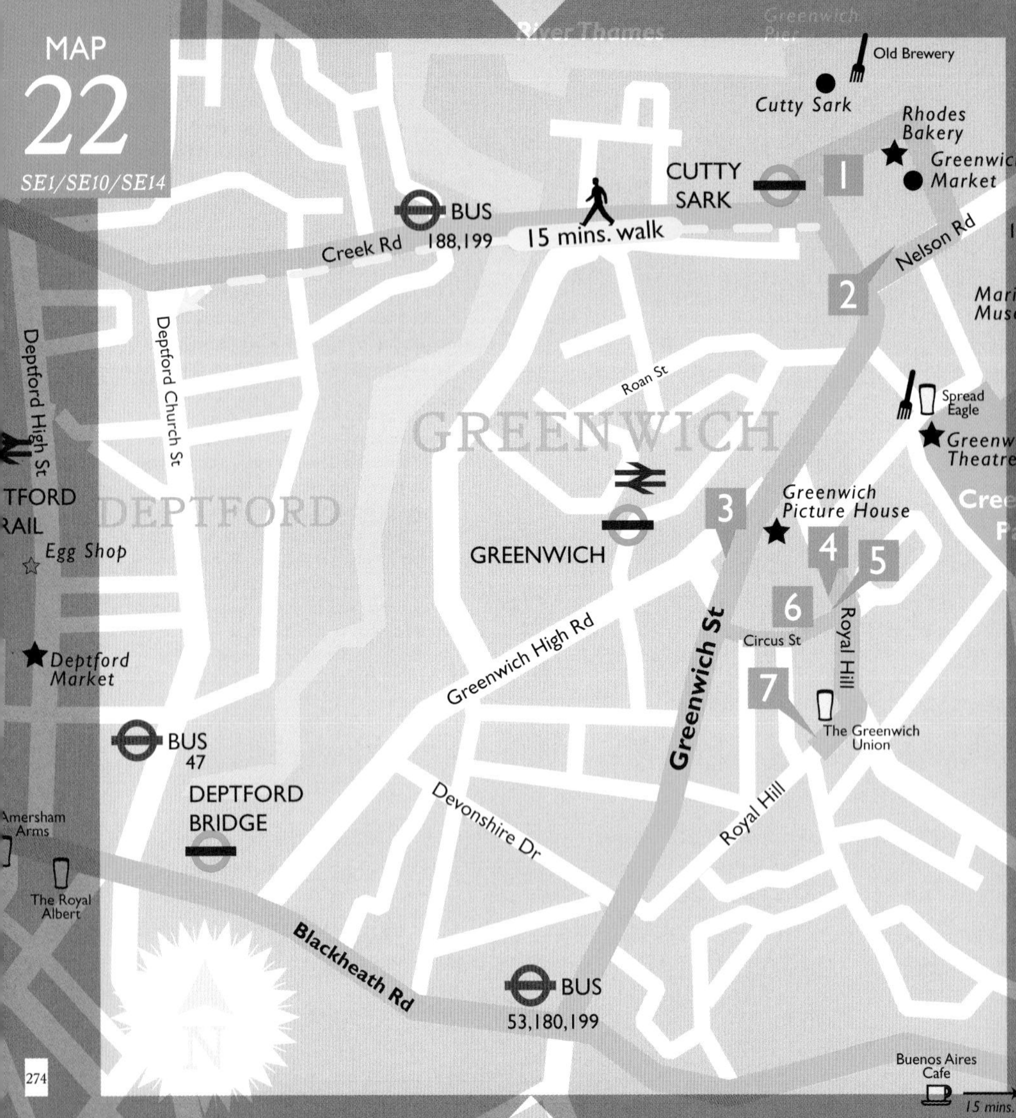

MAP
22
SE1/SE10/SE14
River Thames
Greenwich Pier
Old Brewery
Cutty Sark
Rhodes Bakery
Greenwich Market
CUTTY SARK
1
BUS
188,199
15 mins. walk
Creek Rd
Nelson Rd
2
Deptford Church St
Deptford High St
Roan St
Spread Eagle
GREENWICH
Greenwich Picture House
3
GREENWICH
4
5
6
Circus St
Royal Hill
DEPTFORD
Egg Shop
Greenwich High Rd
Greenwich St
Deptford Market
7
The Greenwich Union
BUS
47
DEPTFORD BRIDGE
Devonshire Dr
Royal Hill
Blackheath Rd
BUS
53,180,199
The Royal Albert
Buenos Aires Cafe
15 mins.

MAP
23
SE22
EAST
DULWICH
BUS
40,176,185,484
Grove Vale
Goose Green
East Dulwi
Scooped
Ice cream
8
Deli
9 mins. walk
Cheese
Crawthew Grove
East Dulwich Grove
BUS
37
EAST DULWICH
Melbourne Grove
Ashbourne Grove
£
Nuffield Rd
BUS
40,176,185
New Cross Rd
Blue
Mountain
Lordship Lane
9
10
11
Blackwater St
Bawdale Rd
LaChandalier

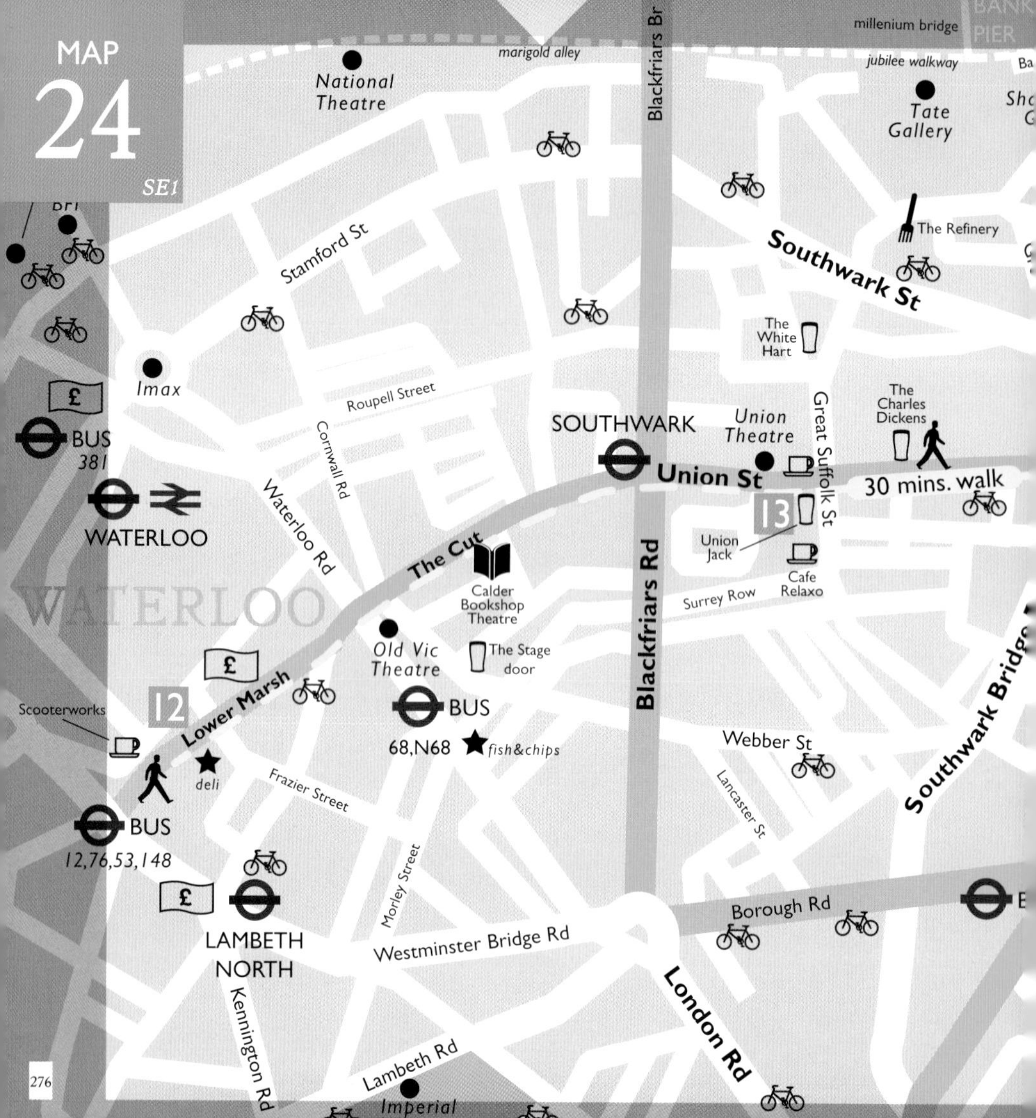
MAP
24
SE1
National Theatre
marigold alley
Blackfriars Br
millenium bridge
BANK PIER
jubilee walkway
Tate Gallery
The Refinery
Southwark St
Stamford St
The White Hart
Imax
Roupell Street
Cornwall Rd
SOUTHWARK
Union Theatre
Great Suffolk St
The Charles Dickens
BUS
381
Union St
30 mins. walk
WATERLOO
Waterloo Rd
13
Union Jack
The Cut
Calder Bookshop Theatre
Blackfriars Rd
Surrey Row
Cafe Relaxo
WATERLOO
Old Vic Theatre
The Stage door
12
Lower Marsh
BUS
Scooterworks
68,N68
fish&chips
deli
Webber St
Southwark Bridge
Frazier Street
Lancaster St
BUS
12,76,53,148
Morley Street
Borough Rd
LAMBETH NORTH
Westminster Bridge Rd
London Rd
Kennington Rd
Lambeth Rd
Imperial

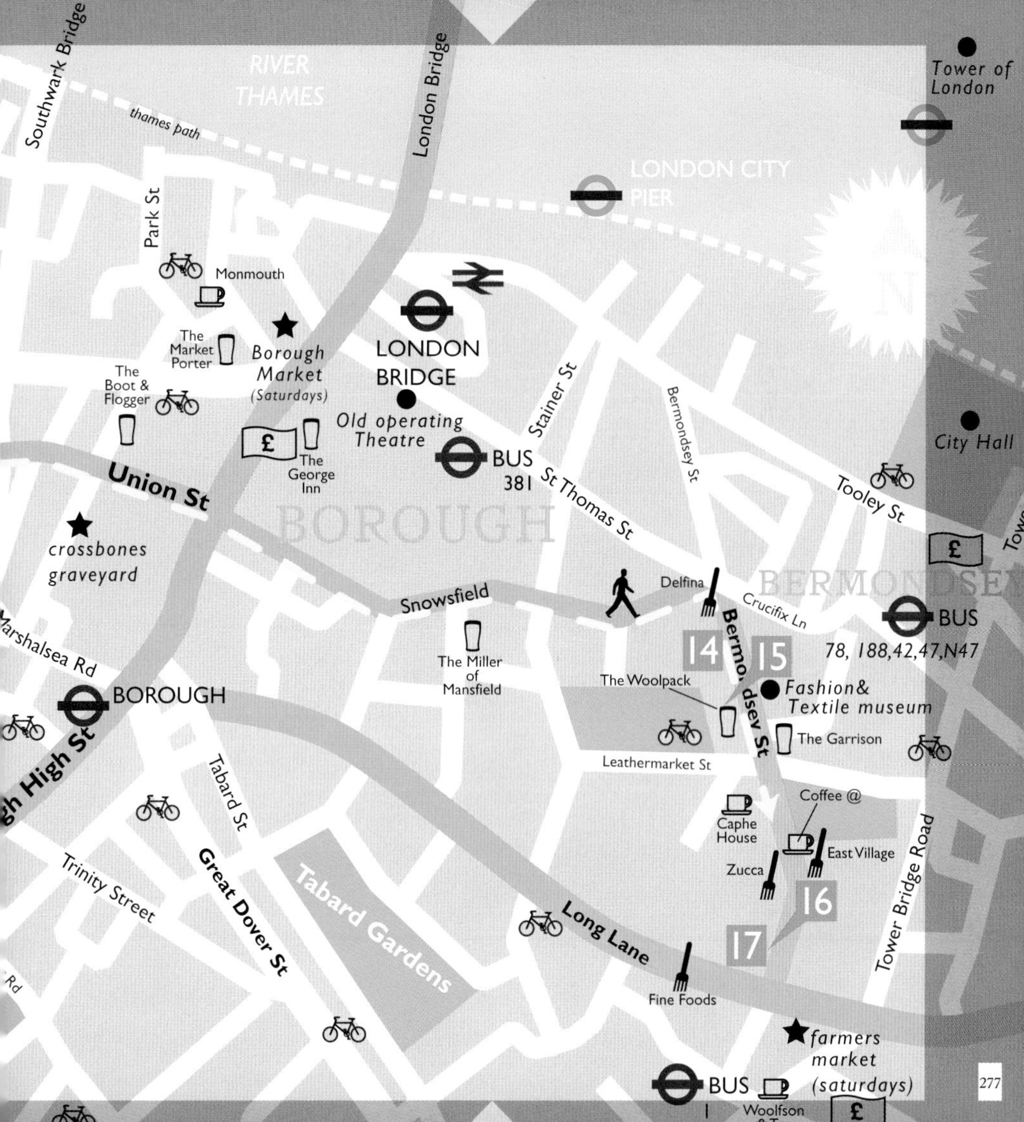

Southwark Bridge
RIVER THAMES
thames path
London Bridge
Tower of London
LONDON CITY PIER
Park St
Monmouth
The Market Porter
Borough Market (Saturdays)
LONDON BRIDGE
The Boot & Flogger
Old operating Theatre
The George Inn
BUS 381
Stainer St
Bermondsey St
City Hall
Union St
BOROUGH
St Thomas St
Tooley St
crossbones graveyard
Delfina
Crucifix Ln
BERMONDSEY
Snowsfield
BUS
78, 188,42,47,N47
Marshalsea Rd
The Miller of Mansfield
14
15
Bermondsey St
The Woolpack
Fashion& Textile museum
BOROUGH
The Garrison
Leathermarket St
Borough High St
Tabard St
Coffee @
Caphe House
East Village
Zucca
Trinity Street
Great Dover St
Tabard Gardens
16
17
Tower Bridge Road
Long Lane
Fine Foods
farmers market (saturdays)
BUS
Woolfson

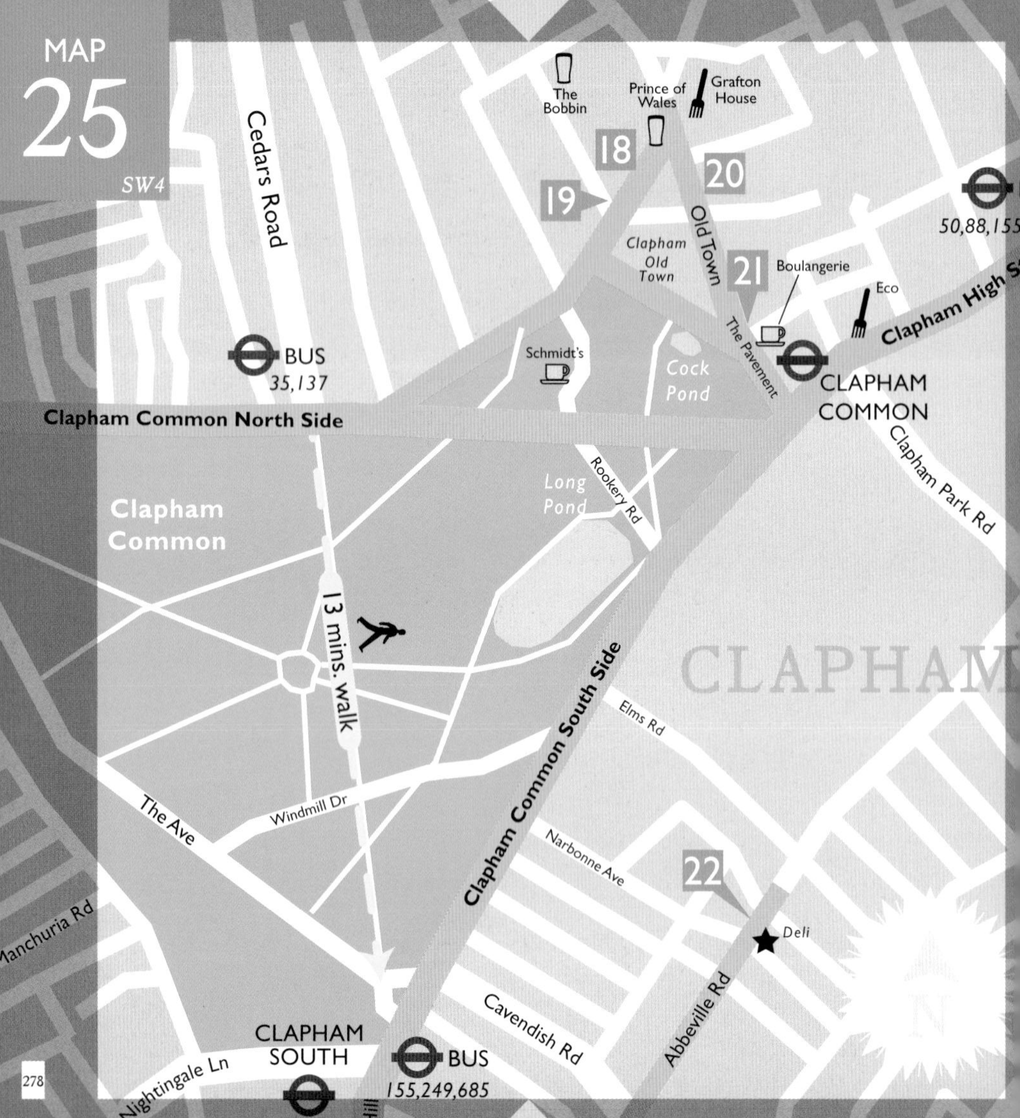
MAP
25
SW4
The Bobbin
Prince of Wales
Grafton House
18
19
20
21
22
Cedars Road
Old Town
Clapham Old Town
Boulangerie
Eco
Clapham High St
50,88,155
BUS
35,137
Schmidt's
Cock Pond
The Pavement
CLAPHAM COMMON
Clapham Common North Side
Clapham Park Rd
Long Pond
Rookery Rd
Clapham Common
13 mins. walk
CLAPHAM
Clapham Common South Side
Elms Rd
The Ave
Windmill Dr
Narbonne Ave
Deli
Manchuria Rd
Cavendish Rd
Abbeville Rd
CLAPHAM SOUTH
BUS
155,249,685
Nightingale Ln

Index *according to shop category*

Acknowledgements and **thank you's**

Reviewers

Penny Blood
Dimi Gaidatzi
Rebecca Lori
Fiona Mcdonald
Tanis Taylor
Geraldine Turvey

Design

Adrian Philpott / PHILPOTT Design
www.philpottdesign.com

Other text

Moritz Steiger

Photography

Moritz Steiger and Effie Fotaki

Published by **MONSTERMEDIA**

independentlondon.com
guide@independentlondon.com

Many thanks to all the shops who gave their support in the making of this book and to all those sending their shop tips and for the direct support of whom we would like to thank by name, David McHugh and John Scott, without whose help this book would not have been possible.

This book is our small contribution to support independent shops and we hope support local high streets for the benefit of local communities.

...and we shall also pat ourselves on the back and give each other a big hug for getting through and achieving what has been our toughest project so far. Phew! Love to Effie.

We hope you like it.

…and finally a big thank you must go out to Hackney Council for their vigor and lack of support while persecuting traffic and parking fines while we tried to go about our business.

Thanks to Brompton Bicycle for their support. www.brompton.co.uk

John Scott (Shop campaigner)

I have always loved small shops. My mother gave 2 1/2 (old) pence for a large white from the local baker. Now many of us are in a hurry, "money rich time poor" = large supermarkets. Small shops are the essence of conviviality, we talk to one another in our Farmers Market, but never in Tesco.

Money is also a curse. An international multiple shop let at £1 million p.a. is worth £30 million (30 x the rent). The same area of 10 smaller shops at £800,000 is only worth £16 m (20 x its rent). So also, old Fred dies, having a pension from his small independent shop tenant of £8,000 pa in rent. His son lets it to an estate agent at £20,000 p.a.

The Howard de Walden estate is a glorious exception to the tyranny of short term greed. Andrew Ashenden created the acclaimed High Street as the finest shopping street in Britain. Small quality shops – *La Fromagerie* and the *Ginger Pig* were brought in from Borough Market – and the most aggressive supermarkets kept out. Notting Hill has been ruined by lack of control of the 'use clause order'. So we are drowned in a plethora of estate agents, bureau de change and fast food/coffee shops. Stricter control would greatly encourage a good varied tenant mix and lower rents. But in the end only good and determined shoppers can save small shops and enjoy them!

John Scott
Founder & Project Leader
Notting Hill Gate Improvement Group

Be
You.
Be Independent
independentlondon.com